The Speeay Sneaky Chef

Quick, Healthy Fixes for Your Family's
Favorite Packaged Foods

MISSY CHASE LAPINE

RUNNING PRESS
PHILADELPHIA • LONDON

Books published by Running Press are available at special discounts for bulk purchases in the United States by corporations, institutions, and other organizations. For more information, please contact the Special Markets Department at the Perseus Books Group, 2300 Chestnut Street, Suite 200, Philadelphia, PA 19103, or call (800) 810-4145, ext. 5000, or e-mail special.markets@perseusbooks.com.

ISBN 978-0-7624-4329-1
Library of Congress Control Number: 2011940237

E-book ISBN 978-0-7624-4361-1

9   8   7   6   5   4   3   2   1
Digit on the right indicates the number of this printing

Cover design by Bill Jones
Interior design by Alicia Freile
Edited by Jennifer Kasius
Cover photo and food photography by Jerry Errico
Food styling by Brian Preston-Campbell
Typography: Garth Graphic, Monotype Sorts, Sassoon and Zapf Dingbats

Running Press Book Publishers
2300 Chestnut Street
Philadelphia, PA 19103-4371

Visit us on the web!
www.runningpress.com

Medical Disclaimer: The ideas, methods, and suggestions contained in this book are not intended to replace the advice of a nutritionist, doctor, or other trained health professional. You should consult your doctor before adopting the methods of this book. Any additions to or changes in a diet or exercise program are at the reader's discretion.

To all you Sneaky Chefs: thank you for trusting me with your families' meals. You inspire me every day . . . and with all my love always to Rick, Emily, and Samantha.

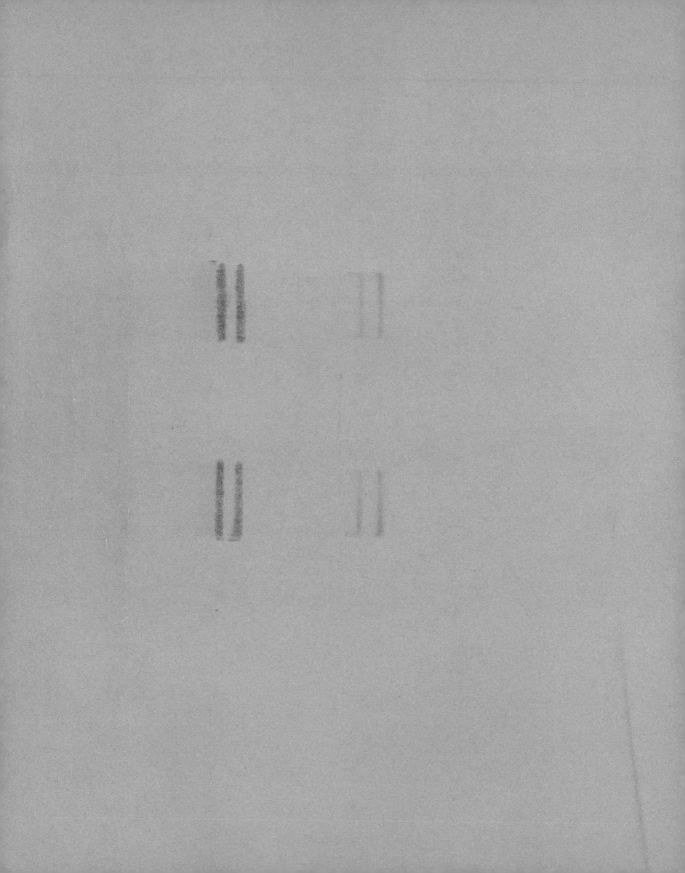

Table of Contents

LUNCH RECIPES

Chapter Seven: Quick, Healthy Fixes for Your Favorite Packaged Foods 221

CHAPTER ONE

Get on the Sneaky Chef Express!

It's a weekday evening and I'm standing in my kitchen. Our pooches Princess and Buddie are chasing each other around the island, my daughter Emily is looking for a notebook she needs for her homework, and her sister Samantha is finishing violin practice—with gusto. Everyone, including my husband Rick, is starving, the clock is ticking, and I am just about to see if I can find something deep in the bottom of the freezer to shove in the microwave, or failing that, to pick up the phone for takeout, when I stop myself. *I'm the Sneaky Chef,* for crying out loud! I've written five books on how to feed families healthfully and deliciously. I dream in menu plans, can recite nutritious shopping lists by heart, and have a pantry that's stocked with good-for-you choices. But what I don't have is *time.*

Time has become the rarest of commodities. Time to spend together as a family, time away from gadgets and gizmos, time for a good night's sleep, and the biggest challenge of them all, even for me, time to prepare healthy meals that your whole family will actually love. And here's the rub: there are actually plenty of quick and easy ways to put meals on the table. After all, the food industry caters to our instant-gratification world. Packaged goods take up 75 percent of the space on supermarket shelves and ready-to-make foods are projected to soon be a 19-*billion*-dollar-a-year business.

Plus, our kids love these familiar brands. They get hooked on how they taste—and how they look. (I bet you know at least one kid who prefers neon-colored mac 'n' cheese from a powder, over the gooey, baked real-cheese version you've slaved over.)

Quick meals kids will gobble up are at our fingertips, so why not use them? The problem is that *convenience often compromises nutrition.* If you're in a hurry and not paying close attention, the processed foods you're likely to buy will be loaded with excess calories, sodium, fat, and sugar. Often what's fast is unhealthy and unsatisfying. In the end, the time you save just won't be worth it.

Don't throw in the kitchen towel yet. I don't spend my days with my Sneaky Chef hat on for nothing—it *is* possible to use these prepared and packaged foods to our good-for-you advantage. This book, *The Speedy Sneaky Chef*, is a three-way balancing act between nutritional ideals, kids' likes and dislikes, and the real-life demands on our time. The answer to our time-crunch is an extension of my tried-and-true philosophy: put extra healthy ingredients into the *packaged and prepared foods* your kids already love. They'll eat it, and you'll be the only one who knows that they're getting a boost of crucial vitamins, minerals, fiber, omega-3s and more. It's Sneaky Chef supercharged *and* superfast!

Looking for recipes that will delight both parents and kids? This book boasts more than 80 all-new dishes that will appeal to your entire family *and* to your busy lifestyle by using packaged goods to speed things up in the kitchen. Plus, they are packed with hidden superfoods like whole grains, fruits, and veggies. They offer you one-meal solutions, so that you won't have to cater to each family member's likes or dislikes like a short-order cook who's short on time. Better yet, you and your spouse won't feel like you're always eating from the kiddie menu either. Plus, these all-new recipes are dense in nutrients, while reducing calories, fat, sodium, and sugars, thereby keeping you and your family full longer so you don't experience a blood sugar "spike and crash."

Ideally, all of our family meals would be made from fresh, local, "scratch" ingredients. But how often does that truly happen? Instead of beating ourselves up for not reaching that goal—or putting off even attempting it until we have "more" time—we can recognize that the ideal isn't always doable. Luckily, the sneaky solutions found in this book will fit into your busy day, and by using them, you'll be living a guilt-free *and* healthier life, no matter how few free minutes you may have.

Why You Want to Get on the Fast-Track to Healthy Eating

Nearly half of all our children's calories come from junk food, according to the National Cancer Institute. Childhood obesity is a growing concern to parents across the country. In fact, First Lady Michelle Obama has squarely put her efforts toward educating children and parents about healthy choices. The USDA's recently revised dietary guidelines emphasize that the gap between their recommendations and what Americans actually eat has never been wider. As a nation, Americans young and old consume far fewer vegetables, fruits, high-fiber whole grains, low-fat milk and milk products than we should. Instead, our plates are filled with much too much added sugars, solid fats, refined grains, and sodium. The USDA found that a full 35 percent of our calories now come from added sugars and solid fats. We can't ignore the fact that what's often on our plates harms us, but we can also have confidence in knowing we can make small changes that will mean big benefits to our loved ones.

You Asked for It!

The thing I like most about my job is hearing from my smart, loyal, and determined readers, who always keep their families' health and happiness at the fore. Some of my most popular recipes are my quick fixes for things like brownies and mac 'n' cheese. So much so that my inbox has been overflowing with pleas for quick fixes to other foods found on readers' supermarket shelves:

"I love your books! I have two of them and my 18-month-old twins enjoy the food. We especially like the quick fixes for pancake and cake mixes. What about store-bought premade cookie mixes? Sugar cookies are a favorite cookie of my kids and my husband (me too for that matter), so I would love to healthify them."

—Lisa L.

"I have a very picky 4-year-old. I've been sneaking purees into the limited foods he will eat for several months now with much success. He loves 'plain' pancakes and waffles for breakfast. Do you have any suggestions for adding purees to basic box mixes? I'm hoping if I can start with something he loves already, I can build on it!"

—Lorie M.

"My girls love buttered noodles from a package. I am able to sneak in the white bean puree, but I would love to know if you have a way of replicating the taste/texture by using whole-wheat noodles and real ingredients. I don't know how 'unhealthy' these packaged noodles are, but I know there has to be a better version of them."

—Natalie G.

If You Can't Beat 'Em, Join 'Em

When my girls were little, it was easy to have some control over what they ate—I was the one loading up their plates. But now that they are old enough to be spending significant time at their friends' houses, they end up munching on things I wouldn't necessarily serve. Apparently, everything tastes better at a friend's house! In Emily's and Sammy's eyes, my standbys are boooooring compared to what their friend Sofie's mom whips up.

Not only that, but just as their tastes in clothes and music and TV shows start to mirror their peers', so too do their choices in food. They've become brand conscious already, and don't always want the homemade version of things. (I suspect there are days when their homemade lunches get swapped for their friends' highly processed, high-fat foods that I'm not willing to give them—I end up inadvertently making other people's kids healthier than my own!)

Recently, Emily came home from a sleepover at her friend Rebecca's house and said that her dad had made the fluffiest, best pancakes in the world. I'm always on the hunt for crowd-pleasing recipes, so I called to ask if he'd share his secret. An old family recipe? Something from the pages of a glossy magazine? Swiped from a TV cooking show? Nope. You guessed it—these pancakes came from a boxed mix. I had to chuckle.

Next time I was at the market, I bought that same exact brand and made pancakes according to the directions on the box. "Thanks Mom, but these tasted better at Rebecca's house," Emily said between bites. Next time, I added some healthy ingredients but made sure not to mess with the texture. The verdict? "Mom these are sooooo much better than before. Not as good as Rebecca's dad's, but better."

Our kids are going to want foods that are not only familiar, but they also want foods their friends are eating—and nine times out of ten those foods are prepackaged. The good news is you *can* give them what they want, without compromising their health. Stock your pantry with many of the same things found in your neighbor's house, but stuff those dishes with good-for-you, undetectable ingredients. They'll clean their plates, and you can rest easy.

NEWS FLASH: THE FOOD INDUSTRY CAN BE AN ALLY

The food industry is listening to concerned parents and responding. Thanks to moms like you who have demanded healthier choices, there have been some really incredible advances in packaged foods. I take advantage of them all. I've said it many times: I am not a purist. If a product has nutritious merit, and my kids will eat it, I'll use it, no matter who produced it. For example, I get tired of constantly fighting the brown vs. white battle with my kids. So when, say, Uncle Ben's® comes out with a fantastic innovation, like "Whole Grain White Rice," with all the nutrition and benefits of brown rice and all the looks and taste of white rice, that's a win-win. Same with "whole grain white bread" and pastas. Kids like it. I like it. No more fights.

Major food manufacturers have started to sneak in healthy foods now, too, like Mott's Medleys® with hidden carrots in the apple juice or Chef Boyardee's® Ravioli with a full serving of completely hidden veggies right in the sauce. This is news a Sneaky Chef can really get behind! Why not push this progress even further by sneaking your own fresh, wholesome foods into these products for a double dose of superfoods?

Plus, we no longer have to go to hunt for healthy or organic foods in specialty stores anymore. Most mainstream supermarkets are now carrying an assortment of good-for-you, natural foods. By being a smart consumer you can reap the benefits of what your supermarket shelves have to offer *and* inject them with your own yummy, healthy touches. In fact, I've already done the legwork for you by navigating the market, researching ingredient lists, scouring nutritional labels, and flagging the best possible products to use as shortcuts. All you'll have to do is flip the pages of this book to reap the benefits.

IT'S NOT ALL ABOUT THE CLOCK

The Speedy Sneaky Chef is true to its title, but it's not just about saving time. It's also about making the moments your family sits around the table meaningful. Sure, the health of your family is a huge priority, but at the core of my sneaky method is the peace it brings to the family table by eliminating the nightly battle over eating veggies, clearing the way for happy, fun memories.

These recipes not only increase the healthfulness of the packaged goods you prepare, but they also give them a homemade feeling. You can add your own personal flair for a taste your kids will try to replicate when *they* are parents. Sure you can dump brownie mix into a bowl, add an egg and call it a day. But using *Speedy*

Sneaky Chef methods, you're adding a bit of care along with hidden superfoods. My readers tell me over and over that they love knowing they've created something you can't get anywhere but home: health-boosting meals, made with love.

GIVE YOURSELF (AND YOUR FOOD PROCESSOR) A BREAK

One of the Sneaky Chef's core methods has been to rely on homemade purees: fruit, veggie, and beans. It's easy to whip up enough for a month of recipes in little over an hour. Still, I'm nothing if not a perfectionist and my goal is to make your life even easier, by saving you even *more* time. So you'll see shortcuts sprinkled throughout this book. A perfect example: starting with frozen cauliflower to make my signature White Puree eliminates the need to wash, chop, and steam it, since it's are already parboiled. (As with most frozen veggies, they are also packed within 24 hours of harvest, which preserves maximum nutrition.) Not to mention the fact that you can use baby food in place of many of my purees—making sneaking as easy as opening a jar!

Win the Eat-Right Race!

The Sneaky Speedy Chef is not only about saving you time, it's also about sharing what I've learned over the course of writing five cookbooks—spilling all the secret tips and tricks I've discovered during the course of creating and testing thousands of recipes myself, and hearing feedback from countless readers every day. I couldn't do it without you. It's fitting, though. We as parents are all in this together. We all want the same thing: to give our growing kids a foundation of health, an appetite for life, and family time that is free from squabbles and filled with fun. Dig in!

CHAPTER TWO

The Sneaky Chef Cheat Sheet

As many busy moms know, the key to saving time is to plan ahead. This chapter will briskly (because I know you've got lots to do) walk you through the Sneaky Chef philosophy and explain the core methods to hiding good-for-you foods in dishes your kids will love.

For some readers, this information will be familiar, and for others who are cracking open my books for the first time, it will be brand new. What makes this book—and the all-new, family-pleasing recipes that follow—different from the rest is that the focus is on giving you the tools and tricks to make healthy meals even when you're in a hurry. Which, I know, seems like *always*, right?

SNEAKY—AND SNAPPY—STAPLES TO KEEP IN THE KITCHEN

Stock your pantry, fridge, and freezer with the following items and you'll be ready to cook up any healthy Sneaky Chef recipe, in an instant! Copy this Sneaky Chef Master Shopping List so you always have it in your purse:

FRESH PRODUCE

- [ ] Baby spinach
- [ ] Zucchini
- [ ] Broccoli
- [ ] Sweet potatoes (or yams)
- [ ] Cauliflower
- [ ] Berries, in season
- [ ] Bananas
- [ ] Avocados
- [ ] Onions
- [ ] Russet potatoes
- [ ] Lemons

MEAT/FISH

- [ ] Beef, lean ground (ideally "grass fed")
- [ ] Turkey, lean ground
- [ ] Hot dogs (no nitrates)
- [ ] Fish fillets—salmon, tilapia, or flounder (ideally not farm-raised)
- [ ] Chicken—skinless, boneless, thinly sliced breasts and tenders

CEREALS/FLOUR

- [ ] Wheat germ, unsweetened
- [ ] Oat bran
- [ ] Rolled oats, old-fashioned
- [ ] Rolled oats, quick-cooking

- [ ] Instant oatmeal packets, variety flavor
- [ ] Whole-grain Cream of Wheat® packets
- [ ] Shredded Mini-Wheats®
- [ ] Cereal, high-fiber flakes
- [ ] Cereal, brown rice
- [ ] Flour, whole wheat (stone ground)
- [ ] Flour, white (unbleached)
- [ ] Whole-grain "pastry" flour
- [ ] Pancake mix, whole grain
- [ ] Corn muffin mix, ideally whole grain
- [ ] Cornmeal
- [ ] Flaxseed, ground

RICE/PASTA

- [ ] Macaroni and cheese, boxed (ideally whole grain and without artificial colors)
- [ ] Whole-grain pasta, elbows, and ziti
- [ ] Lasagna noodles, "no boil"
- [ ] Wonton wrappers
- [ ] Whole-grain white rice
- [ ] Brown rice
- [ ] Quinoa

BREAD

- [ ] Bread, whole wheat
- [ ] Bread crumbs, whole wheat
- [ ] Tortillas, whole wheat
- [ ] Tortillas, corn
- [ ] Pita bread, whole wheat, pocketless
- [ ] Bagels, whole wheat

CANNED GOODS

- [ ] Garbanzo beans (chickpeas)
- [ ] White beans (butter beans, navy, or cannellini)
- [ ] Refried beans, low-fat, vegetarian
- [ ] Baked beans, vegetarian
- [ ] Sardines, in water, skinless and boneless
- [ ] Tuna, in water (preferably "chunk light")
- [ ] Tomatoes, plum, whole
- [ ] Tomato paste
- [ ] Tomato soup, ideally low-sodium
- [ ] Evaporated skim milk

JARS/BOTTLES

- [ ] Baby foods—especially sweet potatoes, carrots, peas, zucchini, garden vegetables, prunes, plums, apricots, blueberries, spinach, squash, and broccoli
- [ ] Pomegranate juice
- [ ] Salsa
- [ ] Applesauce
- [ ] Ranch dressing (no MSG)
- [ ] Ketchup
- [ ] Marinara sauce
- [ ] Tomato sauce
- [ ] Jam, no sugar added

FROZEN FOODS

- [ ] Blueberries (without added syrup or sweeteners)
- [ ] Strawberries (without added syrup or sweeteners)
- [ ] Cherries (without added syrup or sweeteners)
- [ ] Green peas, sweet
- [ ] Corn, yellow, off cob
- [ ] Edamame (soybeans in shell or shelled)
- [ ] Frozen pureed butternut squash
- [ ] Cauliflower florets
- [ ] Broccoli florets
- [ ] Onions, chopped

NUTS/OILS

- [ ] Almonds, blanched and slivered
- [ ] Walnuts
- [ ] Extra virgin olive oil
- [ ] Canola oil
- [ ] Cooking oil, spray

TEA/COCOA

- [ ] Cocoa, unsweetened
- [ ] Green and herbal teas, decaffeinated

DESSERTS

- [ ] Chocolate chips, semisweet
- [ ] Gelatin, unflavored
- [ ] Chocolate syrup
- [ ] Whipped cream, spray can
- [ ] Frozen yogurt, low-fat

DAIRY/EGGS

- [ ] Yogurt, low-fat, plain
- [ ] Yogurt, low-fat, Greek style
- [ ] Cheese, shredded, reduced-fat cheddar
- [ ] Cheese, shredded, reduced-fat Mexican blend
- [ ] Cheese, shredded, reduced-fat Italian blend

- [ ] American cheese slices, 2% milk
- [ ] Parmesan cheese
- [ ] Ricotta cheese, part skim
- [ ] Tofu, firm block
- [ ] Eggs (with added omega-3)
- [ ] Powdered milk, nonfat

OTHER

- [ ] Chicken broth, boxed (no MSG), ideally low-sodium
- [ ] Vegetable broth, boxed, (no MSG), ideally low-sodium
- [ ] Cinnamon
- [ ] Honey
- [ ] Pure maple syrup
- [ ] Pure vanilla extract
- [ ] Baking powder, nonaluminum
- [ ] Baking soda
- [ ] Powdered sugar
- [ ] Brown sugar
- [ ] Raw or Turbinado sugar
- [ ] Lentils (dried or canned)
- [ ] Hummus
- [ ] Italian seasoning
- [ ] Taco seasoning (no MSG)
- [ ] Chili powder

Plus, Remember These Rapid Rules

In a rush? Here are a few shortcuts that will make figuring out what items to put in your basket a snap!

1. Choose items that have five or less ingredients listed.
2. Scan the first three ingredients named (manufacturers have to list them in order of quantity). Look for the words "100 percent" or "whole" when it comes to grains and juices, and avoid "white flour" and "enriched."
3. If a label lists "high-fructose corn syrup" or "partially hydrogenated oil" (trans fats), leave it on the shelf.
4. Always opt for the low-sodium version (better to add your own salt, if desired).
5. Can't pronounce the ingredients? Skip it.
6. Aim for foods that have 3 grams or more of fiber per serving.
7. Take a pass on anything that says it's got more than 12 grams of sugar per serving.
8. Frozen is better than canned. Fresh, in season produce trumps all.

THE SNEAKY CHEF'S BAG OF TRICKS: 14 METHODS OF DISGUISE

If you've got a picky eater (or two!) pulling up a chair to your table, the following methods will become your secret weapon for enticing them to eat nutritiously. Your family will be none the wiser that they're enjoying some of the healthiest ingredients around because your meals will look and taste just like their favorites. Only *you* will know what's hidden inside, and just how much of a cinch it is to prepare them.

Method One:
PUREE

When you puree food it becomes much more concentrated, which means it's extremely dense in nutrients, affording you maximum benefits in every bite. I recommend using a blender for pureeing smoothies, ice-based drinks, and soups, since it is better suited to working with liquids or mushy solids than a food processor. That said, a small food processor has the upper hand when pureeing vegetables, since you don't have to add much, if any, water, and you'll end up with a better, less runny puree. (See page 41 for puree recipes.) Increasingly, popular stick or immersion blenders will also work well to make purees.

Method Two:
COMBINE REFINED AND UNREFINED

This book often calls for a packaged "whole-grain *pastry* flour" or white whole-wheat flour, which retains a good deal of the usual texture and weight of white flour while also providing the benefit of fiber, vitamins, and minerals. These days, you can even find whole-grain blend pancake mix, breads, and pastas on the supermarket shelves. These products also provide the advantage of whole grains without sacrificing the look, feel, and taste of white flour.

Method Three:
USE FOODS THAT HIDE WELL

The hallmark of being a Sneaky Chef is the ability to completely hide foods your kids would normally object to into their all-time favorite dishes. The best way to do that is to camouflage the good-for-you ingredient in foods with similar colors and textures. It's crucial, however, that the hidden element either enhances the overall original taste or adds no taste of its own. It's also important that the look or texture doesn't change. Finally, the golden rule of sneakiness: *What you add must be nutritious.* That's why I've included a list of sure-bet superfoods below.

or blueberry juice (a day's worth of vitamin C), or low-fat milk (calcium, vitamin D, and protein).

Method Five:
COMBINE FOODS THAT ARE A SPECIFIC NUTRITIONAL COMPLEMENT TO EACH OTHER

Method Four:
SUBSTITUTE NUTRITIOUS LIQUID FOR WATER WHEN BOILING FOODS

A true Sneaky Chef never misses a trick—or a chance to inject an extra dose of health into a meal. That's why when a job calls for water, consider using a liquid with more nutritional value and a taste that complements the dish, such as chicken or beef broth (providing minerals and protein), veggie broth (potassium, calcium, and minerals), green tea (immunity-building antioxidants), pomegranate

If you're having trouble getting your kid to eat one healthy dish, getting them to eat two may seem like a fantasy. The good news is that many of the recipes in this book are designed to combine ingredients that either make a more complete protein or help with the absorption by the body of another nutrient, so you can whip up a single dish that does the nutritional duty of two. Talk about multitasking magic!

Method Six:
IDENTIFY FOODS KIDS ARE LIKELY TO ENJOY STRAIGHT UP

Why make your life hard when it doesn't have to be? It may be difficult to believe during a stand-off at the dinner table, but there are actually good-for-you foods that kids will eat without a fight. Offer them snacks like edamame (soybeans), cherries, snap peas, strawberries, corn on the cob, pistachios, sunflower seeds, baby carrots, popcorn, artichokes, whole grapes, roasted chestnuts, and even hummus. Keep in mind that the foods will be more appealing if your child is hungry and if there isn't any junk food around to tempt them. You'll also get better results if they're distracted, if they're with kids their age who'll eat the food without a fuss, or if you're spotted enjoying them— and don't offer to share.

Method Seven:
ALTER THE COOKING METHOD TO AVOID FRYING

Steam, bake, broil, roast, or grill instead of frying. Putting away your deep fryer doesn't mean you have to shelve flavor— or a satisfying crunch. Use these methods to give a recipe the crispiness of fried food, without the added fat: measure the oil with a teaspoon instead of pouring it right out of the bottle; use a pastry brush to baste on the oil or a spray to mist; blast the dish with high heat under the broiler for a minute to crisp the breading; and swap juice or broth for oil.

Method Eight:

CUT THE EFFECTS OF TOXINS OR FATS BY DILUTING THE INGREDIENTS WITH SOMETHING HEALTHIER

Reduce the "junk" factor in your child's favorites by diluting them with something healthy. For example, reduce the mercury levels in a tuna fish sandwich by diluting it with heart-healthy sardines; mix plain yogurt into high-fat creamy salad dressings; substitute fruit, vegetable, or bean puree for butter in baked goods; cut fruit juice with decaffeinated green tea or water; thicken sauces and soups with bean puree. Just be sure that whatever you add doesn't dilute the original taste, and both you and your kid will have a truly happy meal.

Method Nine:

CUT CALORIES AND DOUBLE VOLUME WITH LOW-CAL, NUTRITIOUS "FILLERS"

"Fill 'em up" has an all-new meaning: by adding volume with nutritious ingredients that have fewer calories per portion, such as mixing veggies into your meatballs or pureed cauliflower into your mashed potatoes, you and your family will feel more satisfied with fewer calories. Bulking up works best with ingredients that have a high water and fiber content, like fruits and veggies.

Method Ten:

USE SLOWER-BURNING FOODS TO AVOID A BLOOD SUGAR "SPIKE AND CRASH"

Ever give your child a handful of jellybeans only to see them bounce off the walls before sinking into an overtired meltdown? That's the sugar at work. Refined-sugar foods and carbohydrates like white bread and pastas make your blood sugar shoot up, and may give you a quick burst of energy. But soon after, your blood sugar tends to plummet, leaving you feeling lethargic and even hungrier than before. Complex carbs like whole grains and proteins like beans and legumes, however, take longer to digest and therefore keep your blood sugar, appetite, and energy level steady.

Method Eleven:
USE *VISUAL* DECOYS TO MAKE FOOD LOOK APPEALING AND FUN

Sometimes seeing isn't believing. If kids can't spy the healthy food, they'll eat it, so make use of appealing colors, fun shapes, and surprising sizes to divert their attention from what's really on their plate. Dust powdered sugar on baked goods, serve foods in minisizes or in individual containers like muffin liners, shape food with cookie cutters, or let them "play" with their food by making it "dip-able."

Method Twelve:
USE KID-FRIENDLY *FLAVOR* DECOYS TO DISTRACT KIDS FROM WHAT'S UNDERNEATH

All your efforts will go for naught if the taste of something suspicious pulls back the curtain on your trickery, so make the most of bold flavors that kids love. Include flavors that are strong enough to cover up your covert ops, like cheese, cocoa, chocolate chips, marshmallows, ranch dressing, and, maybe the most valuable decoy in your kitchen, ketchup.

Method Thirteen:
USE KID-FRIENDLY *TEXTURE* DECOYS

In their own way, kids are connoisseurs. Something may look and taste great, but should they detect anything lumpy, gritty, or leafy, their noses will turn up like a gourmet at a drive-through window. If you're worried that a texture will be objectionable to your child, add a decoy texture that they'll approve of: Sprinkles, chocolate chips, cheese, crushed cereal toppings, and raisins are sure to get a four-star review.

Method Fourteen:
SNEAK AND TEACH

Finally, never miss a chance to *sneak and teach*. Now that your family will be eating the world's healthiest superfoods in every bite of their favorite foods, the pressure is off and you can teach good nutrition in a more relaxed environment. So go ahead and serve up that bowl of steamed spinach, straight up, and tell your kids why Popeye chose to eat spinach instead of potato chips for building strong muscles!

CHAPTER THREE

Do Everything Faster!

The all-new, sure-to-please recipes in this book are designed to streamline your cooking time so you can spend less time in the kitchen and more time with your family. (Or, dare I say it, doing something just for yourself, like reading a book or having lunch with a friend.)

There are other ways to make meal prep a breeze, and over the years, I've collected these lists of quick tips that will help you shake a leg in the supermarket, hustle at home, and rustle up recipes in no time flat.

If you only remember one trick, it's this: NEVER GO TO THE MARKET WITHOUT A SHOPPING LIST! Sounds pretty elementary, but I know we've all been in such a mad dash to get out the door that we don't always stop to jot down what we need. (Or even more maddening, we *do* write it down, but leave it on the kitchen counter.) But these days, there are plenty of ways to keep a running list on us at all times thanks to smart phones, apps, spreadsheets, and online shopping sites. (Be sure to copy the Sneaky Chef Master Shopping List on pages 22–24)

How to Get In and Out of the Supermarket in a Flash

1. Have a snack before you go because if you shop hungry, you'll end up tossing a lot of random, unnecessary, unhealthy impulse buys in your cart.

2. Try to leave your kids at home! While I love to do almost everything with my girls, grocery shopping is an exception.

3. Organize your shopping list by where the items are in the store, or list them by category so you can skim the list easily. It helps to visualize yourself walking through the market as you jot down the items you need.

4. Don't bite off more than you can chew. Plan for at least 3 days worth of meals per visit. Any less will have you back in the store too soon and any more doesn't allow for an unexpected change in your daily schedule.

5. Go on off hours. Weekends and weekday shopping during rush hour (5 to 7 p.m.) are usually the busiest times, while Tuesday and Wednesday mornings are quietest. Don't bother with Monday morning as stores are just getting deliveries and the shelves aren't restocked yet.

6. Save yourself some brainpower and time by using the "unit price" that's on the shelves. This will save you from having to calculate which product is the better value. (The lower the unit price, the more economical the item is.)

7. Stick to the perimeter of the store to find the healthiest and freshest items: produce, dairy, deli, meats, and frozen foods.

8. Only walk up an aisle if you have to—you'll be less likely to buy something you don't need.

9. Be loyal. If you become a regular at one supermarket, you'll get familiar with its layout and won't waste time searching for things.

Can't Leave the Kids at Home?

My readers have some great tips on how to navigate the supermarket with little ones.

"I load my cell phone with cartoons. It keeps my son occupied so I can concentrate on shopping."

—Dawn R.

"I pack a small snack for my 2-year-old and try to go first thing in the morning when it's not crowded and when she's well rested. Having her with me helps me not to linger in the aisles myself!"

—Jackie

"We cut pictures out of flyers and paste them to my list. That way the kids can help me. If it's not on the page, it doesn't go in the cart."

—Jillian M.

"If I do take my kids to the store, I give my 9-year-old the list and let him mark off what we've already put in the cart. I also ask him to tell me what's next on the list. It keeps him occupied and prevents him from fighting with his little sister!"

—Stacey

9 Ways to Get Through the Checkout Line More Quickly

1. Organize your items on the conveyor belt by category, so that all the frozen and refrigerated foods end up in the same bags.

2. Bring your own large, reusable bags. They hold more, which means fewer trips from your car to your kitchen. (Be sure to clean them with an antibacterial wipe occasionally.)

3. Bag your own groceries so you can group them properly.

4. Spot someone with a ton of coupons in front of you? Hightail it to another line.

5. If the lines are long, ask the manager to open another checkout line—most are happy to oblige.

6. Counterintuitive as it is, express lanes aren't always faster. Time studies show you're better off behind one person with more items than behind several people with fewer items.

7. If you can help it, never shop the day before a long weekend, holiday, or snow storm.

8. Be friendly and get to know your cashiers so you can steer your cart to the most seasoned one. He or she will move more swiftly and won't get bogged down with price checks.

9. Self-checkout is only faster in theory.

Make Unloading Groceries a Snap

1. For the days you don't have time to make multiple trips from your car to your kitchen (or when it's rainy or cold), store a folding shopping cart in your trunk, so you can load it up and make only one trip.

2. When loading the car, place the cold items in your trunk last so they're the first things you unpack. At home, stash away the frozen items first, the refrigerated ones next, and the pantry items last.

3. As much as it'd be nice to have help, if you put the groceries away yourself,

you'll know where everything is, saving you time later. (You can also label the shelves so other people can follow your plan.)

14 Quick-fire Tips for Making Healthy Meals

1. Double your recipe and freeze half for down the line, or put it in a lunch box in the fridge for the next day. Or, choose one day a month and cook and freeze many meals at a time.

2. Choose a different kind of grain each week and cook a few batches. Rice, pasta, quinoa, and barley can keep in the refrigerator for up to 3 days.

3. Make twice as much of your morning smoothie and save the rest in the freezer or a popsicle mold for a sweet treat later.

4. When you get home from the store, wash and chop an entire head of lettuce, and store it in a sealed plastic bag in the fridge. Do the same with the veggies you won't use right away and stash them in the freezer in plastic freezer bags, so you can quickly toss them in soups, omelets, chili, etc.

5. Raise the oven temperature by 25 degrees to speed up the cooking time of most dishes. (Warning: This does not work with baking.)

6. Use a toaster oven when possible—it takes less time to preheat and often cooks faster than the oven.

7. Cover items in the microwave with a wet paper towel, which will help the food cook faster and eliminates any splattering you'll have to clean up later.

8. Read the entire recipe through before you begin cooking.

9. Take meat and fish out of the fridge 30 minutes before you cook it so it can come to room temperature.

10. Don't forget to preheat the oven while you're prepping the meal.

11. Chop potatoes and veggies smaller to cook faster.

12. Eat more fish—it's the fastest cooking animal protein!

13. Load your blender the night before with smoothie ingredients; add ice and blend in the morning.

14. Make muffins or quick bread and freeze; defrost the night before.

MAXIMIZE YOUR PANTRY/FRIDGE IN 10 EASY STEPS

1. Group like items together so it takes less time to find everything.

2. Use a lazy Susan or two for spices and bottled foods.

3. Store small, loose items in clear containers.

4. Shift new items to the back and older items to front.

5. Create an eye-level snack shelf of healthy treats your kids can grab on their own.

6. Keep less healthy items out of kids' view by keeping them on a higher shelf or turning the packages sideways so your kids don't see the label.

7. Check for and discard outdated items on a regular basis.

8. Leave meats in a plastic grocery bag and store them on the bottom shelf so that they don't drip on anything.

9. The "use by" dates on the container aren't always accurate once the item is opened, so use a marker to write the date you opened jars, tubs, boxed broth, etc. and keep track yourself.

10. Freeze food in portion sizes so you don't waste food and time breaking them apart.

By now you know all my time-saving secrets! So why delay? Turn the page for some delicious, good-for-your-whole family recipes!

JUST A FEW NOTES BEFORE WE BEGIN

1. All the purees can be frozen for up to three months and kept in the refrigerator for up to three days.

2. The truly skillful Sneaky Chef sneaks up on the family with these methods.

That is to say, she uses less than my recommended amount of puree called for in each recipe for the first few times to acclimate their taste. You don't want to raise a red flag by overloading a dish with a new taste or texture. Instead, over time, gradually increase the amount of the booster, only adding as much as you can get away with.

3. For all the purees, it's ideal to use frozen fruit and vegetables, especially to cut down on prep time. (Frozen means blanched, so you simply need to thaw, plus they're already chopped and washed for you.) The fact that they are frozen right after they're picked ensures that a great deal of the vitamins and minerals have been locked in. I actually prefer frozen to fresh blueberries for just that reason. The "fresh" blueberries have sometimes been picked up to ten days before you buy them, whereas the frozen might have been picked the same day they were processed. (The only exception here is spinach. I strongly advise using only raw baby spinach, not frozen, because fresh young leaves will give you a much better taste and won't affect the overall flavor or texture of the recipe.)

4. You'll notice a stopwatch at the top of many recipes. This indicates the approximate cooking time for the recipe (not counting the prep time, which is also designed to be minimal). If there's no stopwatch, there's no cooking time.

5. The best advice I can give the Speedy Sneaky Chef is to "cook once, eat twice." Make double your recipes and freeze half for another day. This is an invaluable trick that always comes in handy in a pinch!

6. The "Optional Extra Boost" at the bottom of many recipes is an ingredient that will add more nutrition, but I can't really classify it as disguised and invisible. Your kids will pick up on it, so make sure they like this flavor or texture before adding it. Otherwise, you run the risk of ruining the entire dish.

CHAPTER FOUR

Make-Ahead Purees

The recipes that follow are the cornerstone of my Sneaky Chef recipes. These purees and blends are made of superfoods, fruits, veggies, grains, beans, and nuts that are packed with essential nutrients, which will give your whole family a good-for-you boost. Slip them into the meals and treats your kids love to eat—without them even realizing they are there. In this book you'll be able to hide them in dozens of packaged and prepared foods, getting you in and out of the kitchen faster.

Best yet, each of these purees takes less than 10 minutes to whip up. Find just a few minutes each week to make the ones you plan to use later. All you need is a food processor or a blender. (If you use a blender, keep in mind you may have to add a bit more liquid than the recipes call for.) You can store the purees and blends in the fridge for up to 3 days and in the freezer for up to 3 months. I recommend stashing them in ¼-cup sizes so you won't have to worry about defrosting too much or too little when you're ready to use them. Zip-top freezer bags work well for storing purees, or covered ice cube trays are a good size as well. (Please note, that I've tinkered with these a bit since my last book and have eliminated lemon juice from my Purple, Green, and White Purees.)

Healthy cooking will be a breeze!

Sneaky Timesaver:

Some healthy Make-Ahead purees are actually unwittingly prepared for you by the food industry. If you find yourself short on time, or if you're in the midst of a recipe and you don't have a Make-Ahead on hand, the purees used in this book can be substituted with baby foods and other store-bought purees. Each recipe includes a list of Instant Substitutes.

Make-Ahead Recipe #1: Purple Puree*

3 cups raw baby spinach
    leaves**

1½ cups fresh or frozen
    blueberries, no added
    syrup or sugar

1 to 2 tablespoons water

Note: I've tinkered with this a bit since my last book and have eliminated lemon juice from the recipe.

**Note: I prefer raw baby spinach to frozen spinach for this recipe for its more mild flavor; if you must use frozen spinach, only use 1 cup.*

Raw baby spinach should be rinsed well, even if the package says "prewashed." If you're using frozen blueberries, give them a quick rinse under cold water to thaw a little, and then drain.

Place the spinach in the food processor first and pulse a few times. This will reduce the spinach significantly. Next add the blueberries and 1 tablespoon of water; puree on high until as smooth as possible. Stop occasionally to push the contents to the bottom. If necessary, use another tablespoon of water to create a smooth puree.

This recipe makes about 1 cup of puree; double it if you want to store another cup. It will keep in the refrigerator up to 3 days, or you can freeze ¼-cup portions in sealed plastic bags or small plastic containers.

Top reasons to eat blueberries

✓ They're packed with more antioxidants than any other fruit or vegetable.

✓ Blueberries contain 38 percent more heart-healthy anthocyanins than red wine.

✓ They boost lutein which helps protect vision.

✓ Blueberries help neurons in the brain talk to each other, significantly improving learning function, motor skills, and memory.

✓ Like cranberries, they also help protect against urinary tract infections.

✓ They can help relieve both diarrhea and constipation.

Top reasons to eat spinach

✓ Calorie for calorie, leafy greens like spinach provide more nutrients than almost any other food.

✓ Spinach is an excellent source of antioxidants, including vitamin C, vitamin E, beta-carotene, and manganese.

✓ One-half cup of cooked spinach contains a whopping 500 percent of the daily recommended value of bone-strengthening vitamin K.

✓ Spinach has twice as much fiber as other greens.

✓ It flaunts 13 flavonoids that help to fight cancer and prevent heart disease.

INSTANT SUBSTITUTES FOR PURPLE PUREE:

- Blueberry, blueberry/apple, or blueberry/pear baby food, stage 1 or 2
- Prune baby food, stage 1 or 2
- Blueberry applesauce

Purple Puree is used in the following recipes:

Make-'Em-in-Minutes Mini Muffins

Smoky Joe Sliders

Anyone-Can-Make Crepes—Chocolate

In-a-Hurry Brownie Cookies

Lickety-Split Layer Cake

Make-Ahead Recipe #2: Orange Puree

1 medium sweet potato or
    yam, peeled and coarsely
    chopped

3 medium to large carrots,
    peeled and sliced into
    thick chunks

2 to 3 tablespoons water

Place the carrots and sweet potatoes in a medium-sized pot and cover with cold water. Bring to a boil and cook for about 20 minutes, until carrots are very tender. Careful—if the carrots aren't tender enough, they may leave telltale little nuggets of vegetables in recipes, which will reveal their presence to your kids—a gigantic no-no for the Sneaky Chef.

Drain the carrots and sweet potatoes and put them in the food processor with 2 tablespoons of water. Puree on high until smooth—no pieces of vegetables showing. Stop occasionally to push the contents to the bottom. If necessary, use another tablespoon of water to smooth out the puree, but the less water, the better.

This recipe makes about 2 cups of puree; double it if you want to store more. Orange Puree will keep in the refrigerator for up to 3 days, or you can freeze ¼-cup portions in sealed plastic bags or small plastic containers.

Top reasons to eat sweet potatoes
✓ These bright veggies contain twice as much fiber
    as white potatoes, causing it to rank lower on
    the glycemic index.
✓ They stabilize blood sugar.

✓ Sweet potatoes' vivid orange color indicates significant amount of the plant pigment beta-carotene, which reduces the risk of lung cancer by protecting against secondhand smoke and pollution and also converts to vitamin A in the body in order to help skin stay clear and smooth.

✓ They're one of the best sources of "feel-better," mood-lifting complex carbs.

Top reasons to eat carrots

✓ They're a rich source of beta-carotene and carotenoids, which protect vision, especially night blindness.

✓ Studies suggest that as little as one carrot per day could cut your risk of lung cancer in half, especially for children who are around second-hand smoke.

✓ Carrots are a good source of fiber, which helps with digestion and lowering cholesterol.

✓ They're also a great source of vitamin A and beta-carotene, which are important for healthy skin, eyes, hair, growth, and resisting infections.

✓ Tip: Cook them with a little fat to help absorption of their carotenoids.

INSTANT SUBSTITUTES FOR ORANGE PUREE:

- Carrot and/or sweet potato baby food, stage 1 or 2

Orange Puree is used in the following recipes:

Banana Breakfast Quick Bread

Pumpkin Breakfast Quick Bread

PB&J Pancake Sticks

In-a-Wink Waffle Sandwiches

Breakfast Banana Dog

Pumpkin Pie Hot Cereal

Roll-Out-the-Door Cheese Omelet

Banango Breakfast Popsicles

Hot Cocoa Breakfast Popsicles

BBQ Chicken Mac 'n' Cheese

Presto Pizza Mac 'n' Cheese

Parmesan Chicken Fries

Rapid Ravioli Soup

Cheesy Chicken Lunchbox Muffins

Turkey Club Sub

Meatball Calzone

No-Bake Peanut Butter Bar

Miso Noodle Bowl

Easy Cheesy Chicken Nachos

Chicken Parm Pops

Quicker-Than-Take-Out Chinese
   Orange Chicken

Sweet Salmon Sliders

Crunchy Panko Meatballs

Swift Spaghetti & Meatball Pizza

No-Boil Baked Ziti

Ridiculously Easy Ravioli Lasagna

Butterscotch Crisps

Chocolate Chip Cookie Cake

Anyone-Can-Make Crepes—Strawberry

Chocolate Peanut Butter Cup Candies

Banana Pops

Make-Ahead Recipe #3: Green Puree*

MAKES ABOUT 2 CUPS OF PUREE

2 cups raw baby spinach
   leaves**

2 cups broccoli florets,
   fresh or frozen

1 cup sweet green peas,
   frozen

2 to 3 tablespoons water

*Note: I've tinkered with
this a bit since my last
book and have eliminated
lemon juice from the
recipe.

**Note: I prefer raw baby
spinach to frozen spinach
for this recipe for its more
mild flavor; if you must
use frozen spinach, only
use 1 cup.

Sneaky Timesaver:

I recommend using frozen broccoli florets
(with no added sauce) which are frozen at
the peak of freshness to preserve maximum
nutrients and have been blanched before freezing.
The florets simply need to be thawed or microwaved
for a minute before pureeing—it saves time chopping,
washing, and steaming fresh broccoli.

Raw baby spinach should be rinsed well, even if the package
says "prewashed."

To prepare Green Puree on the stovetop, pour about 2
inches of water into a pot with a tight-fitting lid. Put a vegetable
steamer basket into the pot, add the broccoli, and steam for
about 10 minutes, until very tender. Add the frozen peas to the
basket for the last 2 minutes of steaming. Drain.

To prepare in the microwave, place the fresh broccoli in a
microwave-safe bowl, cover with water, and microwave on high
for 8 to 10 minutes (frozen florets take only 1 to 2 minutes),
until very tender. Add peas for last 2 minutes of cooking. Drain.

Place the raw spinach in the food processor first and pulse
a few times. This will reduce the spinach significantly. Next

add the cooked broccoli and peas, along with 2 tablespoons of water. Puree on high until as smooth as possible. Stop occasionally to push the contents to the bottom. If necessary, use another tablespoon of water to make a smooth puree.

This recipe makes about 2 cups of puree; double it if you want to store more. Green Puree will keep in the refrigerator for up to 3 days, or you can freeze ¼-cup portions in sealed plastic bags or small plastic containers.

Top reasons to eat peas
✓ Peas are one of the least contaminated conventionally grown foods.
✓ They are readily available and convenient year-round in the frozen section.
✓ Peas boast twice the protein of most veggies or legumes.
✓ They're loaded with health-supportive antioxidants and anti-inflammatory nutrients including vitamins C and E, which also boost immunity.
✓ Peas have a ton of fiber and protein which are associated with a lowered risk of type 2 diabetes.

✓ They're a rich source of vitamin B_1 (thiamin), which is essential for energy production, nerve function, and carbohydrate metabolism.

Top reasons to eat broccoli
✓ Numerous studies confirm this cruciferous powerhouse is an effective cancer-fighter.
✓ Broccoli is rich in both soluble and insoluble fiber, which helps reduce cholesterol and aids digestion.
✓ It helps regulate insulin and blood sugar.
✓ Broccoli is one of the top 10 omega-3 essential fatty acid plant foods.
✓ It's loaded with antioxidants and compounds that boost immunity against illness and protect against heart disease.
✓ Broccoli contains bone-building calcium, which helps fight osteoporosis.

Top reasons to eat spinach

✓ Calorie for calorie, leafy greens like spinach provide more nutrients than almost any other food.

✓ Spinach is an excellent source of antioxidants, including vitamin C, vitamin E, beta-carotene, and manganese.

✓ One-half cup of cooked spinach contains a whopping 500 percent of the daily recommended value of bone-strengthening vitamin K.

✓ Spinach has twice as much fiber as other greens.

✓ It flaunts 13 flavonoids that help to fight cancer and prevent heart disease.

INSTANT SUBSTITUTES FOR GREEN PUREE:

• Mixed garden vegetables baby food, stage 2
• Spinach and potatoes baby food, stage 2
• Green beans and rice baby food, stage 2

Green Puree is used in the following recipes:

California Roll Bowl

Too-Good-to-Be-True Taquitos

Oops the Wontons Fell Apart Soup

Easy-to-Do BBQ Chicken Pizza

Crunchy Fish Stick Tacos

Mini Muffin Tin Meatballs

Chili Fusilli

Make-Ahead Recipe #4: White Puree*

MAKES ABOUT 2 CUPS OF PUREE

2 cups cauliflower florets, fresh or frozen (about ½ a small head)

2 small to medium zucchini, peeled and coarsely chopped

1 to 2 tablespoons water, if necessary

Note: I've tinkered with this a bit since my last book and have eliminated lemon juice from the recipe.

Sneaky Timesaver:

I recommend using frozen cauliflower florets (with no added sauce) which are frozen at the peak of freshness to preserve maximum nutrients and have been blanched before freezing. They simply need to be thawed or microwaved for a minute before pureeing—it saves time chopping, washing, and steaming fresh cauliflower.

To prepare White Puree on the stovetop, pour about 2 inches of water into a pot with a tight-fitting lid. Put a vegetable steamer basket into the pot, add the cauliflower, and steam for about 10 minutes, until very tender. Drain.

To prepare in microwave, place the cauliflower in a microwave-safe bowl, cover it with water, and microwave on high for 8 to 10 minutes (frozen florets take only 1 to 2 minutes), or until very tender. Drain.

Meanwhile, place the raw peeled zucchini in your food processor and pulse a few times. Next add the cooked cauliflower and 1 tablespoon of water to the food processor (work in batches if necessary) and puree on high until smooth. Stop occasionally to push the contents to the bottom. If necessary, use another tablespoon of water make a smooth puree, but the less water, the better.

This recipe makes about 2 cups of puree; double it if you want to store more. It will keep in the refrigerator for up to 3 days, or you can freeze ¼-cup portions in sealed plastic bags or small plastic containers.

Top reasons to eat cauliflower

✓ It's one of the top 10 omega-3 essential fatty acid plant foods.

✓ Cauliflower is a member of the cruciferous vegetable family, known cancer-fighters.

✓ Its low-calorie, high-nutrient density makes it a good weight management aid.

✓ It's an excellent source of antioxidant and immune-boosting vitamin C and manganese, both of which reduce the risk of cardiovascular diseases and cancer.

✓ Cauliflower contains many anti-inflammatory substances which reduce arthritis and lower the risk of inflammatory diseases.

✓ It's also a good source of fiber and aids digestion.

✓ It has glucoraphanin, which protects the stomach lining, reducing the risk of stomach ulcers and cancer.

Top reasons to eat zucchini

✓ One cup of zucchini has 36 calories and 10 percent of the recommended daily amount of dietary fiber, which aids in digestion, prevents constipation, maintains low blood sugar, and curbs overeating.

✓ Zucchini contains Vitamin C, which helps the immune system and reduces such conditions as asthma and bruising.

✓ It's Mother Nature's gift to dieters: very low in calories and no fat.

✓ This veggie is a good source of energy-boosting potassium, which is also a heart-friendly electrolyte that helps regulate blood pressure and counters the effects of sodium.

INSTANT SUBSTITUTES FOR WHITE PUREE:

• Butternut or winter squash baby food, stage 1 or 2

• Frozen pureed butternut or winter squash (no added ingredients)

Note: These substitutes have a stronger flavor than the white puree, so be careful when adding to recipe.

White Puree is used in the following recipes:

BBQ Chicken Mac 'n' Cheese

Chicken Parm Soup

Pita Triangles with Cheesy Pizza Dip

Hushh Puppy Muffins

Meatball Calzone

Quick Quinoa Bean Burrito

Easy-to-Do BBQ Chicken Pizza

Creamy Chicken Risotto Cakes

Texas Two-Step Tortillas

Chicken Sausage Skillet

Swift Shrimp Teriyaki Kebobs

Crunchy Panko Meatballs

Swift Spaghetti & Meatball Pizza

Deep Dish Tortellini Alfredo

No-Boil Baked Ziti

Ridiculously Easy Ravioli Lasagna

Better-for-You Black & White
    Cupcakes

Make-Ahead Recipe #5: White Bean Puree

MAKES ABOUT 1 CUP OF PUREE

1 (15-ounce) can white
    beans* (Great Northern,
    navy, butter, or cannellini)
1 to 2 tablespoons water

*Note: If you prefer to use
whole beans, soak overnight
and cook as directed.*

Rinse and drain the beans and place them in the bowl of your food processor. Add 1 tablespoon of the water, then pulse on high until you have a smooth puree. If necessary, use a little more water, a tiny bit at a time, until the mixture smoothes out and no pieces or full beans are visible.

This recipe makes about 1 cup of puree; double it if you want to store another cup. It will keep in the refrigerator for up to 3 days, or you can freeze ¼-cup portions in sealed plastic bags or small plastic containers.

{ Sneaky shortcut }

No time to take your food processor off the shelf? Just mash the beans using a fork.

Top reasons to eat white beans
✓ They're rich in vitamin B, folate, and magnesium, which protects the heart.
✓ White beans are a good source of high-quality, low-calorie, low-fat plant protein.
✓ They help curb cravings, which is important for weight control.
✓ They give long lasting, slow-burning energy.

✓ White beans help control blood sugar and reduce the risk of diabetes.
✓ They're loaded with fiber to make you feel full longer and help with digestion.

INSTANT SUBSTITUTES FOR WHITE BEAN PUREE:

• Store-bought hummus
• Vegetarian refried pinto beans
Note: These substitutions only work for savory recipes—not desserts!

Quick Tip:

Other useful instant supermarket purees are tomato paste, applesauce, unsweetened fruit spread, and fresh, ripe avocados (mashed) or guacamole.

White Bean Puree is used in the following recipes:

On-the-Go Brown Sugar Breakfast
   Cookies
Chocolate Banana Cream Pie
   Sneak-Wich

Valentine's Soup
Super Simple Microwave Lasagna
Tuna Penne Alla Vodka
Light 'n' Lemony Pound Cake

Host a Sneaky Chef Puree Party!

Want to have fun with your friends while you're doing something healthy for everyone's family? Gather a group of sneaky conspirators, serve some snacks (healthy ones, of course), put on some music, and combine forces to whip up a whole month's supply of Sneaky Chef purees. Each person takes charge of making up a batch of one puree for the whole group. By the time you're finished, everyone will go home with a nice assortment of purees that can be used in dozens of recipes. It's quick, it's easy, and with your pals around, it won't feel like work at all.

BASIC INGREDIENTS FOR PARTY:

- Friends and family (ideally four to sixteen people)
- Food processors (one for about every three people; some people will be washing and chopping while others are processing)
- Fresh or frozen fruit/vegetables (each person chooses a puree and brings the ingredients)
- Good music
- Bottle of wine (optional)

WHO DOES WHAT:

- Some people rinse produce
- A few take charge of chopping
- Others set up areas for each puree (green, purple, orange, white, white bean)
- One person runs each food processor
- Several people bag cup portions of each puree
- Others label each bag with the name of the puree and the date it was prepared (always a good idea when you're storing something in the freezer)

CHAPTER FIVE

Make-Ahead "Instant" Mixes

Sure, your grocery store shelves are fully stocked with quick, instant mixes for cakes, cookies, and pancakes that are crowd pleasers. And of course, you could spend a whole afternoon making a cake completely from scratch. But the following recipes offer a middle ground—homemade mixes you can keep on hand for when you're short on time, but want to keep an eye on nutrition.

Store-bought mixes simply offer the right ratio of dry ingredients so all you have to do is add the wet ingredients—they're truly fail-safe. Their downfall is that they're predominantly made of re-fined white flour and tons of sugar. (The whole grain mixes on the shelves today are not very palatable, hard-to-find, and generally heavy, not pleasing products.) They're also packed with preservatives and stabilizers.

These instant substitutes for store-bought mixes take the good (convenience, taste, texture) and combine it with the healthfulness of a whole-grain product. The "blend" of whole and refined grains (see Method Two, page 26) introduces benefits without losing the integrity, taste, and texture of the light and familiar cakes, pancakes, and cookies we all know and love.

By making my own mixes, I was able to reduce the sugar by a significant amount and still retain the great taste. Not only that, but they're generally less expensive than the store brands.

You'll see that in many cases, I call for a base of "whole-grain *pastry* flour," an innovative new entry in the world of baking. Compared to heavy, whole-grain flour, whole-grain pastry flour is refined in a way that gives us the benefit of fluffier, lighter texture and taste, with the nutritional benefits of the vitamins and fiber of whole-grain flour. If you don't live near a major natural foods market, you can easily order this flour online—try arrowheadmills.com or bobsredmill.com.

You'll also notice some recipes call for pure vanilla *powder* (not extract). This can usually be found at speciality stores like Williams-Sonoma and Sur La Table. Or consult the Nielsen-Massey website (nielsenmassey.com).

I keep a stash of dry mixes in my fridge, ready to throw into a quick home-made batch of cookies for a block party or a stack of blueberry pancakes after a sleepover. Funny thing is, the kids seem to love these versions even better than the packaged versions—and they take the same amount of time. Another delicious win-win!

Make-Ahead "Instant" Recipe #1:
Pancake and Waffle Mix

4½ cups whole-grain "pastry" flour or white whole-wheat flour

¾ cup wheat germ

¼ cup sugar or raw sugar

2 teaspoons kosher salt

2 tablespoons baking powder

Optional: **2 tablespoons** pure vanilla powder

Place all ingredients in a plastic bag or airtight container, seal, shake, and store in refrigerator until ready to use.

Nutrition Burst

Whole-Wheat Flour

Manganese, magnesium, tryptophan, and fiber make whole-wheat flour a powerful addition to any recipe. It helps to regulate digestion and keeps your blood sugar at an even keel.

Pancake and Waffe Mix is used in:

On-the-Go Bbrown Sugar Breakfast Cookies

PB&J Pancake Sticks

Black Forest Pancakes

Super Blueberry Waffles

Butterscotch Crisps

Anyone-Can-Make Crepes

Make-Ahead "Instant" Recipe #2:
Banana Quick Bread and Muffin Mix

3 cups whole-grain "pastry" flour or white whole-wheat flour

1½ cups brown sugar, packed

1 cup dry banana flakes or dry oatmeal and banana cereal or baby food

1 teaspoon cinnamon

1 teaspoon kosher salt

1½ teaspoons baking soda

2 teaspoons baking powder

Place all ingredients in a plastic bag or airtight container, seal, shake, and store in refrigerator until ready to use.

Banana Quick Bread and Muffin Mix is used in:

Banana Breakfast Quick Bread

Make-Ahead "Instant" Recipe #3:
Pumpkin Quick Bread and Muffin Mix

3 cups whole-grain "pastry" flour or white whole-wheat flour

1½ cups brown sugar, packed

3 teaspoons pumpkin pie spice

1 teaspoon kosher salt

1½ teaspoons baking soda

2 teaspoons baking powder

Place all ingredients in a plastic bag or airtight container, seal, shake, and store in refrigerator until ready to use.

Pumpkin Quick Bread and Muffin Mix is used in:

Pumpkin Breakfast Quick Bread

Make-Ahead "Instant" Recipe #4:
Whole-Grain Muffin Mix

4 cups whole-grain "pastry"
flour or white whole-
wheat flour

1 cup quick-cooking oats

1 cup sugar

1 teaspoon salt

2 teaspoons baking soda

1 tablespoon baking powder

For chocolate muffins only:

½ cup unsweetened
cocoa powder

Place all ingredients in a plastic bag or airtight container, seal, shake, and store in refrigerator until ready to use.

Whole Grain Muffin Mix is used in:

Make-'Em-in-Minutes Mini Muffins

Make-Ahead "Instant" Recipe #5:
Chocolate Chip Cookie Mix

4½ cups whole-grain "pastry" flour or white whole-wheat flour

1 cup white, unbleached sugar

1 cup brown sugar, packed

2 teaspoons kosher salt

2 teaspoons baking soda

4 cups semisweet or dark chocolate chips

Optional: 1 tablespoon vanilla powder

Place all ingredients in a plastic bag or airtight container, seal, shake, and store in refrigerator until ready to use.

Chocolate Chip Cookie Mix is used in:

Chocolate Chip Tricky-Treat Cookies   Chocolate Chip Cookie Cake

Make-Ahead "Instant" Recipe #6:
Chocolate Cake Mix

1¾ cups whole-grain "pastry" flour or white whole-wheat flour

¾ cup sugar

½ cup unsweetened cocoa

½ teaspoon cinnamon

¾ teaspoon kosher salt

1 tablespoon baking powder

¼ cup nonfat dry milk

Optional: 1 tablespoon vanilla powder

Place all ingredients in a plastic bag or airtight container, seal, shake, and store in refrigerator until ready to use.

Chocolate Cake Mix is used in:

60-Second Mini Chocolate Cakes   Lickety-Split Layer Cake

BREAKFAST BANANA DOG *Sneaky ingredients:* Flaxseed or wheat germ, carrots, sweet potatoes (p. 95)

OATMEAL BANANA BRÛLÉE *Sneaky ingredients:* Banana, oats, wheat germ (p. 96)

TROPICAL TWIST BREAKFAST ICE-CREAM CONES *Sneaky ingredients:* Mango, strawberries, banana (p. 109)

HOT COCOA BREAKFAST POPSICLES *Sneaky ingredients:* Carrots, sweet potatoes, wheat germ (p. 108)

WAFFLE ICE CREAM SANDWICHES *Sneaky ingredients:* Mixed berries, yogurt, whole grains (p. 105)

PB&J PANCAKE STICKS *Sneaky ingredients:* Carrots, oats, mixed berries, whole grains (p. 88)

ON-THE-GO BROWN SUGAR BREAKFAST COOKIES *Sneaky ingredients:* Whole grains, white beans (p. 84)
MAKE-'EM-IN-MINUTES MINI MUFFINS *Sneaky ingredients:* Spinach, blueberries, whole grains, flaxseed, pomegranate juice (p. 82)

HOT APPLE PIE PARFAIT *Sneaky ingredients:* Flaxseed, wheat germ (p. 111)

Make-Ahead "Instant" Recipe #7:
Yellow Cake Mix

4 cups whole-grain "pastry" flour or white whole-wheat flour

2 cups white, unbleached sugar

1 teaspoon kosher salt

2 tablespoons baking powder

½ cup nonfat dry milk

Optional: 1 tablespoon vanilla powder

Place all ingredients in a plastic bag or airtight container, seal, shake, and store in refrigerator until ready to use.

Yellow Cake Mix is used in:

Better-for-You Black & White Cupcakes

Make-Ahead "Instant" Recipe #8:
Brownie Mix

1½ cups whole-grain "pastry"
   flour or white whole-
   wheat flour
2½ cups brown sugar, packed
¾ cups unsweetened cocoa
1 teaspoon kosher salt
1 tablespoon baking powder
½ cup nonfat dry milk
Optional: 1 tablespoon
   vanilla powder

Place all ingredients in a plastic bag or airtight container, seal, shake, and store in refrigerator until ready to use.

Brownie Mix is used in:

In-a-Hurry Brownie Cookies

Make-Ahead "Instant" Recipe #9:
Tortilla Chips

After seeing how fast, fun, and easy these chips are to make, you'll wonder why anyone buys the kind in the bag. Not only are these crunchy snacks not bad for kids, they are also actually good for them, providing a good source of calcium, iron, and fiber, all for a fraction of the calories and fat of packaged tortilla chips. You can easily vary the shapes by cutting strips instead of triangles, to keep things interesting and new.

12 (6-inch) round corn tortillas (white or yellow)

2 tablespoons extra virgin olive oil

1 teaspoon salt (or seasoning of choice, such as taco seasoning, p.76)

Preheat oven to 400 degrees.

Brush both sides of the tortilla with oil. Stack 6 of them together and, using kitchen shears or scissors, cut the stack into 8 triangles, for a total of 48 chips. Repeat with the final 6 tortillas. Scatter the chips in a single layer onto a large cookie sheet and sprinkle them evenly with salt or seasoning of choice. Bake 10 minutes or until crispy and golden brown.

Tortilla Chips are used in:

Easy Cheesy Chicken Nachos

Make-Ahead "Instant" Recipe #10:
Taco Seasoning

¼ cup chili powder

2 tablespoons *each:* onion powder, garlic powder, paprika, and dried oregano

1 tablespoon ground cumin

1 tablespoon brown sugar, packed

1+ tablespoon kosher salt, to taste

1+ teaspoon crushed red pepper flakes, to taste

Place all ingredients in a plastic bag or airtight container, seal, shake, and store until ready to use.

Taco Seasoning is used in:

Too-Good-to-Be-True Taquitos

Quick Quinoa Bean Burrito

Easy Cheesy Chicken Nachos

CHAPTER SIX

The Speedy Recipes

The stopwatch icon at the top of some recipes indicates the time it takes to cook the dish, once the ingredients have been prepped. I chose not to flag the **total** time (prep and cooking) because I've found it's a number that depends on a few variables: Do you have a make-ahead puree already on hand or do you need to make it for the recipe? Will you substitute a ready-made puree, such as baby food, or prepare a homemade one? All of these factors vastly affect prep time. That said, I designed each recipe to require minimal prep time and as few ingredients as possible. Most recipes in this book should take no longer than 30 minutes, start to finish. The rule of "Cook Once, Eat Twice" makes mealtime a breeze, so whenever you have time, double the recipe and freeze half.

BREAKFAST RECIPES

Banana Breakfast Quick Bread

40 minutes

The cozy and comforting smell of this quick bread wafting through the house is worth the surprisingly minimal effort you'll need to make it. Plus, this recipe covers most of the food pyramid: it's got fruit, veggies, whole grains, eggs, and dairy in one delicious low-fat loaf. Unless you're a particularly early riser, you might want to make this ahead and toast it on busy school mornings. I make a loaf on Sunday evening and it easily lasts for three breakfasts (and a couple of coffee breaks with my neighbors).

MAKES ABOUT 14 SERVINGS

2 large eggs

2 tablespoons canola oil

⅔ cup low-fat vanilla yogurt

½ cup Orange Puree (see Make-Ahead Recipe #2, p. 45) or baby food sweet potato puree

2 large bananas, mashed (about 1 cup)

⅓ cup water

¼ cup wheat germ

One package (about 14 ounces) store-bought banana quick bread mix or 3½ cups Make-Ahead "Instant" Banana Quick Bread and Muffin Mix (p. 60)

Preheat oven to 375 degrees and grease or spray a loaf pan 9 inches by 5 inches or 8 inches by 4 inches with oil.

In a large mixing bowl, whisk together all ingredients except the muffin mix. Add the dry mix and stir until it is fully incorporated into the wet ingredients.

Bake for 40 minutes or until top is lightly browned and until a toothpick inserted in the center comes out clean.

PER SERVING: Calories 179; Total Fat 3.3g; Saturated Fat 0.4g; Trans Fat 0g; Cholesterol 26mg; Sodium 255mg; Carbohydrate 32.8g; Dietary Fiber 2.9g; Sugars 15.9g; Protein 4.1g; Vitamin A 7%; Vitamin C 3%; Calcium 7%; Iron 12%.

Bananas

Perhaps the easiest snack in town, bananas are high in potassium, fiber, vitamin B6, and manganese, and are low in saturated fat, cholesterol, and sodium. Bananas keep your heart healthy, aid digestion, and strengthens your eyes and bones.

Wheat Germ

With plenty of iron, protein, B vitamins, folic acid, vitamin E, zinc, magnesium, manganese, and chromium, wheat germ supports your nervous system and keeps fatigue from running you down.

Pumpkin Breakfast Quick Bread

40 minutes

In this recipe, I've replaced almost all the oil with vegetable puree. I often load up my blender on Sunday evenings, blend all the ingredients, and bake in the morning. Or I make the bread ahead and it keeps all week.

MAKES ABOUT 14 SERVINGS

2 large eggs

2 tablespoons canola oil

¼ cup reduced-fat cottage cheese

⅓ cup Orange Puree (see Make-Ahead Recipe #2, p. 45) or baby food carrot puree

½ cup low-fat milk

¼ cup wheat germ

One package (about 14 ounces) store-bought pumpkin quick bread mix or 3½ cups Make-Ahead "Instant" Pumpkin Quick Bread and Muffin Mix (p. 61)

Preheat oven to 375 degrees and grease or spray a loaf pan 9 inches by 5 inches or 8 inches by 4 inches with oil.

In a large mixing bowl, whisk together all ingredients except the muffin mix. Add the dry mix and stir until it is fully incorporated into the wet ingredients.

Bake for 40 minutes or until top is lightly browned and until a toothpick inserted in the center comes out clean.

PER SERVING: Calories 194; Total Fat 3.6g; Saturated Fat 0.5g; Trans Fat 0g; Cholesterol 132mg; Sodium 343mg; Carbohydrate 35.8g; Dietary Fiber 2.5g; Sugars 19.1g; Protein 4.8g; Vitamin A 9%; Vitamin C 1%; Calcium 8%; Iron 7%.

Make-'Em-in-Minutes Mini Muffins

I was excited to find Duncan Hines® brand of whole-grain muffin mix. I almost missed it in my market because it was shelved with the cake mixes and because its whole grain goodness isn't marked prominently on the box. (If you can't find it in your local store, or if you prefer, you can use your own homemade whole-grain muffin mix on page 62). Make a few batches and freeze these little guys for up to 3 months. Simply zap them in the microwave for a minute to defrost.

MAKES ABOUT 40 MINI MUFFINS OR 13 REGULAR SIZED MUFFINS (3 MINI MUFFINS OR 1 REGULAR MUFFIN PER SERVING)

1 box Duncan Hines® 100% Whole Grain Muffin Mix (20-ounce box) or 3 cups Make-Ahead "Instant" Whole-Grain Muffin Mix (see p. 62)*

¼ cup ground flaxseed

2 large eggs

3 tablespoons canola or vegetable oil

½ cup Purple Puree (see Make-Ahead Recipe #1, p. 43) or baby food blueberry puree**

½ cup pomegranate or blueberry juice

Optional: ½ cup chopped walnuts

*If using Make-Ahead "Instant" Whole Grain Muffin Mix, add ½ cup semisweet chocolate chips to the recipe.

**Pear/blueberry or blueberry/apple puree works just as well.

Preheat oven to 400 degrees and line muffin tins with paper muffin liners or spray with oil.

Empty the muffin mix into a large bowl, breaking up any lumps. Stir in flax, eggs, oil, puree, juice, and walnuts (if using), until fully moistened. Scoop the batter into muffin tins, filling to just below the top.

Bake mini muffins for 14 to 16 minutes, regular sized muffins for 20 to 22 minutes, or until the top of muffins springs back when you press gently with finger.

PER SERVING: Calories 315; Total Fat 7.8g; Saturated Fat 2.0g; Trans Fat 0g; Cholesterol 28mg; Sodium 237mg; Carbohydrate 33.1g; Dietary Fiber 3.9g; Sugars 15.6g; Protein 4.1g; Vitamin A 4%; Vitamin C 0%; Calcium 3%; Iron 4%.

Nutrition Burst

Walnuts

Walnuts are the perfect snack; they're the number one plant source of brain-boosting omega-3 fatty acids, which also reduce inflammation in the body.

On-the-Go Brown Sugar Breakfast Cookies

Ever pour cereal into a bowl only to discover only the dregs had been left in the box? The question of how to make use of that last bit of crushed cereal inspired this yummy treat. The girls gobbled up fiber-rich cereal they'd normally wrinkle their nose at and Rick proclaimed them the best cookies I've ever made, and started eating the batter before I could get the second batch in the oven!

12 minutes

MAKES ABOUT 40 COOKIES

2 cups shredded wheat cereal, plain or lightly frosted

1 teaspoon cinnamon

1 cup whole-grain pancake mix (such as Aunt Jemima® Whole Grain Blend) or 1 cup Make-Ahead "Instant" Pancake and Waffle Mix (p. 59)

8 tablespoons unsalted butter, melted

⅔ cup brown sugar, packed

½ cup White Bean Puree (see Make-Ahead Recipe #5, p. 54)

Optional extra boost: ¼ cup each slivered almonds and raisins

Preheat oven to 400 degrees and line a baking sheet with parchment paper.

Pour shredded wheat into a plastic bag and using a rolling pin or your hands, gently crush cereal into coarse crumbs. Add cinnamon and pancake mix to bag, shake, and set aside.

In a mixing bowl, whisk the melted butter with the brown sugar and White Bean Puree. Add the dry ingredients to the wet and mix just until combined. Mix in optional extras, if using. Drop single tablespoonfuls of batter onto the baking sheet, slightly flattening with your palm, leaving about an inch between each cookie. Bake 10 to 12 minutes, until lightly browned around the edges.

Remove from the pan and let cool. Store in an airtight container or freeze in a sealed plastic bag.

PER SERVING: SERVING SIZE: 2 COOKIES: Calories 120; Total Fat 4.7g; Saturated Fat 2.8g; Trans Fat 0g; Cholesterol 12mg; Sodium 72mg; Carbohydrate 18.1g; Dietary Fiber 1.8g; Sugars 7.7g; Protein 2.1g; Vitamin A 3%; Vitamin C 0%; Calcium 3%; Iron 4%.

Nutrition Burst

Cinnamon

Cinnamon is very effective for balancing blood sugar, especially when added to sweet foods.

Banana Berry Breakfast Crumble

20 minutes

Dessert for breakfast? Sounds decadent, doesn't it? Rest assured, this fast, fruity, and fun dish is healthier than it appears. Plus, it cooks itself while I get the kids' backpacks prepped for the day. All you need for a rich and creamy way to start the morning is five minutes and a toaster oven.

MAKES 4 SERVINGS

2 instant oatmeal packets, any flavor, sweetened

2 tablespoons ground flaxseed

2 cups frozen mixed berries (such as blueberries, blackberries, strawberries, and/or raspberries), unthawed, no added syrup or sugar

1 banana, sliced

4 teaspoons butter, diced

Optional topping: low-fat vanilla or blueberry yogurt

Preheat oven or toaster oven to 400 degrees. Spray 4 individual ramekins with oil, or for one large crisp, spray the bottom and sides of an 8-inch or 9-inch square baking dish.

Empty the oatmeal packets into a mixing bowl and mix in the flax. Place about ½-cup of berries in each individual ramekin, or place all the berries in one baking dish. Add banana slices.

Sprinkle the oat mixture evenly on top of banana and berries, then dot the tops evenly with butter and lightly spray top with cooking spray oil. Bake 15 to 20 minutes until topping is golden brown.

Serve warm, with a dollop of yogurt if desired.

PER SERVING: Calories 174; Total Fat 5.5g; Saturated Fat 2.1g; Trans Fat 0g; Cholesterol 10mg; Sodium 79mg; Carbohydrate 30.3g; Dietary Fiber 6.9g; Sugars 16.4g; Protein 2.0g; Vitamin A 8%; Vitamin C 6%; Calcium 4%; Iron 7%.

{ Sneaky shortcut }

Sneaky shortcut: Take 2 minutes at breakfast to think about what's for dinner. Then take meat or fish out of the freezer to thaw or marinate, or make a quick shopping list before your day gets started.

PB&J Pancake Sticks

Kids love pancakes, but since they are all carbs, they don't usually have enough staying power. These pancakes solve that problem—they're packed with both satisfying protein and good fats as well as healthy whole grains, so your kids will feel fuller long through the morning. These yummy pancakes are also thicker than most, so kids can dip them. They're so good, why limit them to breakfast? I stick them into Emmy's lunchbox instead of her usual sandwich.

6 minutes

MAKES APPROXIMATELY 32 STICKS

1 large egg

½ cup skim milk

⅓ cup Orange Puree (see Make-Ahead Recipe #2, p. 45) or 1 jar (about ⅓ cup) baby food carrot puree

⅓ cup creamy peanut butter

1 cup frozen mixed berries, slightly thawed, no added syrup or sugar

½ cup oats, uncooked

1 cup Make-Ahead "Instant" Pancake and Waffle Mix (p. 59) or 1 cup whole-grain pancake mix (such as Aunt Jemima® Whole Grain Blend)

Dip ideas: yogurt, all-fruit jam, maple syrup, or peanut butter

In a blender, combine all ingredients except pancake mix (and dip ideas) and blend until smooth. Add pancake mix and pulse a few times until the dry ingredients are fully incorporated—mix with a spoon, if necessary. Batter should be fairly thick.

Heat a griddle or large skillet over medium and spray or wipe with oil. Test the pan by tossing in a few drops of water; it will sizzle when it's hot enough. The skillet will grow hotter over time, so turn down the heat if the pan starts to smoke.

Spoon out about one tablespoon of batter onto the skillet, dragging into an elongated or finger-shape rather than round pancakes. When bubbles begin to set around the edges and the skillet-side of each pancake is golden (peek underneath), gently flip over. Continue to cook 2 to 3 minutes or until the pancake is fully set, then remove from pan.

Serve as hand-held pancakes with your favorite dip. Leftover pancakes will keep for 3 days in the refrigerator, or up to 3 months sealed in a plastic bag in the freezer.

PER SERVING: Calories 339; Total Fat 13.8g; Saturated Fat 2.6g; Trans Fat 0g; Cholesterol 62mg; Sodium 493mg; Carbohydrate 42.0g; Dietary Fiber 7.0g; Sugars 8.7g; Protein 13.4g; Vitamin A 19%; Vitamin C 17%; Calcium 13%; Iron 14%.

Black Forest Pancakes

There's just something too good to be true about chocolate pancakes! I still can't believe they're healthy, even though I loaded them up with antioxidant rich cocoa and cherries, and gave them a boost of satiating protein with cottage cheese. The kids thought they were getting away with something by adding chocolate chips. I didn't tell them otherwise.

6 minutes

MAKES APPROXIMATELY 32 PANCAKES

½ cup low-fat chocolate milk

¼ cup low-fat cottage cheese

2 tablespoons unsweetened cocoa

¾ cup fresh or frozen cherries, no added syrup or sweetener, pitted

1 large egg

¾ cup whole-grain pancake mix (such as Aunt Jemima® Whole Grain Blend) or

¾ cup Make-Ahead "Instant" Pancake and Waffle Mix (p. 59)

Optional: ½ cup semisweet chocolate chips

In blender, combine all ingredients except pancake mix (and chocolate chips, if using) and blend until smooth. Add pancake mix and pulse a few times until the dry ingredients are fully incorporated—use a mixing spoon to finish incorporating the dry into the wet batter, if necessary. Mix in chocolate chips, if using.

Heat a griddle or large skillet over medium and spray or wipe with oil. Test the pan by tossing in a few drops of water; it will sizzle when it's hot enough. The skillet will grow hotter over time, so turn down the heat if the pan starts to smoke.

Spoon out about one tablespoon of batter onto the skillet in batches. When bubbles begin to set around the edges and the skillet-side of each pancake is lightly browned (peek underneath), gently flip them over. Continue to cook 2 to 3 minutes or until the pancake is fully set, then remove from pan.

Serve stacked high, drizzled with a little warm maple syrup or dusted with powdered sugar. Place any leftover pancakes in a zip-top bag and store in the freezer for up to 3 months.

PER SERVING: Calories 160; Total Fat 2.9g; Saturated Fat 1.1g; Trans Fat 0g; Cholesterol 148mg; Sodium 368mg; Carbohydrate 26.5g; Dietary Fiber 3.5g; Sugars 9.1g; Protein 7.9g; Vitamin A 3%; Vitamin C 0%; Calcium 10%; Iron 9%.

Quick Tip:

Make these ahead of time and freeze; then toast on weekdays. Or load all wet ingredients in blender the night before and place in refrigerator.

Nutrition Burst

Cherries

With tons of antioxidants, beta-carotene, vitamin C, potassium, magnesium, iron, fiber, and folate, these ruby reds can reduce pain and inflammation and lower your risk for heart disease, diabetes, and some cancers. They may even help you sleep better, too.

In-a-Wink Waffle Sandwiches

By using waffles as the deliciously sweet "bread" to a breakfast sandwich, I was able to add protein to an otherwise all-carb breakfast of waffles and syrup alone. I made these open-faced in the toaster oven in minutes, then closed the sandwiches and gave them to the girls to eat in the car on the way to school. They're so yummy I made one for myself!

MAKES 2 SERVINGS

4 fresh or frozen whole-grain waffles

6 tablespoons Orange Puree (see Make-Ahead Recipe #2, p. 45) or baby food carrot or sweet potato puree

2 slices 2% American cheese

2 slices deli ham

Preheat broiler or toaster oven to high.

Spread one tablespoon of puree on each waffle, then top 2 of the waffles with a slice of ham and cheese. Place all of the waffles in the toaster oven or under broiler, and toast until waffles are lightly browned and cheese is melted. Serve closed, sandwich style.

PER SERVING: Calories 279; Total Fat 11.6g; Saturated Fat 4g; Trans Fat 0g; Cholesterol 25mg; Sodium 970mg; Carbohydrate 31.4g; Dietary Fiber 4g; Sugars 5.4g; Protein 12.4g; Vitamin A 62%; Vitamin C 3%; Calcium 30%; Iron 22%.

Quick Tip:

Avoid eating while behind the wheel. Drivers distracted by eating cause the majority of all car accidents.

Super Blueberry Waffles

4 minutes

It's a funny thing about making homemade waffles—they're actually quicker than homemade pancakes! So long as you have a decent waffle iron, they cook themselves with less effort than standing at a griddle waiting and flipping flapjacks. I make several batches and freeze them in zip-top plastic bags, then presto, toaster waffles any weekday morning!

MAKES 4 WAFFLES

3 tablespoons liquid egg white or
    1 large egg

1 teaspoon pure vanilla extract

¼ teaspoon salt

½ cup applesauce

½ cup baby food blueberry puree or
    blueberry applesauce

¾ cup fresh or frozen blueberries

1 cup whole-grain pancake mix (such as
    Aunt Jemima® Whole Grain Blend) or
    1 cup Make-Ahead "Instant" Pancake
    and Waffle Mix (p. 59)

Low-fat milk, as needed

Maple syrup

Preheat a waffle iron to medium high and spray with oil.

In a large mixing bowl, whisk together the eggs, vanilla, salt, and applesauce. Mix in the puree, blueberries, and pancake mix, adding milk, if needed, to make a fairly thick batter.

Spoon ⅓ to ½ cup batter onto the center of the prepared waffle iron (the amount of batter needed will vary according to the size and type of the waffle iron you're using). Close the top and cook until the waffle is lightly browned, crisp, and lifts easily off the grids, about 3 minutes (or until the indicator light shows ready). Repeat with the remaining batter, spraying the waffle iron with more oil if needed.

Serve immediately as the waffles come off the iron, or keep them warm on a plate, covered with aluminum foil. Serve drizzled with maple syrup.

PER SERVING (2 WAFFLES): Calories 315; Total Fat 1.9g; Saturated Fat 0g; Trans Fat 0g; Cholesterol 0mg; Sodium 738mg; Carbohydrate 61.2 g; Dietary Fiber 8.3g; Sugars 17.6g; Protein 10g; Vitamin A 1%; Vitamin C 24%; Calcium 15%; Iron 12%.

{ *Sneaky shortcut* }

To make your morning breakfast quicker, you can make the batter for any of the sneaky pancake and waffle recipes the night before and leave it covered in the refrigerator overnight.

Breakfast Banana Dog

Sure, you could put banana slices on toast, but what fun would that be? A whole banana on a hot dog bun will not only get your kids giggling, but will also have them gobbling up a breakfast that will get their day started right.

MAKES 1 SERVING

2 teaspoons all-fruit jam

1 teaspoon ground flaxseed or wheat germ

1 teaspoon Orange Puree (see Make-Ahead Recipe #2, p. 45) or baby food carrot puree

1 tablespoon part-skim ricotta cheese

1 hot dog bun, ideally whole wheat or white whole wheat

1 banana, peeled, whole

Optional topping: shredded coconut

In a mixing bowl, combine jam with flax or wheat germ and Orange Puree. Spread ricotta on bun, then some of the jam mixture, and lay down whole banana; top with the remaining jam (to look like ketchup), and shredded coconut, if using (to look like sauerkraut).

PER SERVING: Calories 351; Total Fat 5.8g; Saturated Fat 1.7g; Trans Fat 0g; Cholesterol 8mg; Sodium 360mg; Carbohydrate 67g; Dietary Fiber 9.8g; Sugars 25g; Protein 11g; Vitamin A 7%; Vitamin C 19%; Calcium 11%; Iron 12%.

Oatmeal Banana Brûlée

Someone had given us a crème brûlée kit, which included a small kitchen blowtorch, and we've been caramelizing sugar on top of everything from steamed milk to rice pudding ever since! By adding the sugar to the top rather than mixing it into this brûlée, you'll add sweetness without going overboard. Leave it to the bananas to provide the rest. Best yet, it only takes 5 minutes. (And you don't need a blowtorch—a broiler will work just as well to give this dish a sweet crunch, though the top won't be as hard as the restaurant version which uses way more sugar.)

MAKES 2 SERVINGS

1 ripe banana, peeled

1 cup low-fat milk

½ cup quick-cooking oats

2 tablespoons wheat germ

Dash of cinnamon and salt

2 teaspoons brown sugar, packed

Preheat broiler or toaster oven to high.

Place banana in a pot and roughly mash with the back of a fork or a potato masher. Add the milk, oats, wheat germ, cinnamon, and salt to the pot and bring to a boil. Stir, reduce heat to low, cover, and cook for about 5 minutes until oatmeal has thickened.

Pour into oven-proof ramekins or crocks and top each with about a teaspoon of sugar, spreading evenly over the top. Do not mix in. Place oatmeal under broiler until sugar bubbles and browns slightly, one to two minutes (alternatively, use a kitchen torch to caramelize the tops).

PER SERVING: Calories 226; Total Fat 3.2g; Saturated Fat 1g; Trans Fat 0g; Cholesterol 8mg; Sodium 353mg; Carbohydrate 41.5g; Dietary Fiber 4.5g; Sugars 18.5g; Protein 9g; Vitamin A 6%; Vitamin C 10%; Calcium 15%; Iron 10%.

{ Sneaky shortcut }

Instant oatmeal has about the same nutritional value as the old-fashioned version, so reach for it when you're short on time.

Pumpkin Pie Hot Cereal

If you're a fan of pumpkin pie, this could become your new breakfast staple. It's so delicious, you'll have a hard time convincing yourself how healthy it really is. Combining whole-grain hot cereal packets with canned pure pumpkin puree is a huge upgrade from plain-Jane hot cereal. Plus, the pumpkin pie spice and graham crackers lend this dish an authentic, comforting flavor.

5 minutes

MAKES 2 SERVINGS

2 packets (about ⅔ cup) Instant Healthy Grain Original Cream of Wheat®, unsweetened

6 tablespoons canned 100% pure pumpkin

2 cups low-fat milk

2 tablespoons pure maple syrup

1 teaspoon pumpkin pie spice or cinnamon

⅛ teaspoon salt

2 graham cracker sheets

Add all ingredients *except* the graham crackers into a pot, stir, and bring to a boil. Reduce heat to low, stir, cover, and cook for about 5 minutes until cereal has thickened. Place graham crackers in a plastic bag and using a rolling pin or your hands, gently crush crackers into coarse crumbs. Pour hot cereal mixture into bowls and top each with graham cracker crumbs, spreading evenly over the top.

PER SERVING: Calories 284; Total Fat 4.8g; Saturated Fat 2g; Trans Fat 0g; Cholesterol 10mg; Sodium 368mg; Carbohydrate 52.2g; Dietary Fiber 3.5g; Sugars 29.5g; Protein 11.3g; Vitamin A 135%; Vitamin C 3%; Calcium 39%; Iron 31%.

A note about canned pumpkin:
One of the unsung heroes in the ready-made food world is 100% canned pumpkin. Most of us only think about pumpkin around Thanksgiving, but it's available all-year round, and is an inexpensive, nutrient-dense pantry staple. On its own, pumpkin doesn't have much flavor, which makes it ideal for hiding. It's also an excellent source of the vitally important antioxidant beta-carotene. Fun fact: Did you know pumpkin is a fruit?

Sweetheart Hot Cereal

2 minutes

This 2-minute recipe is perfect for Valentine's Day and everyday! It's about as heart-healthy as you can get with pomegranates and whole grains, and the raspberries do double-duty: not only are they high in fiber, so they help to keep you full, they also provide an excellent antioxidant boost.

MAKES 2 SERVINGS

2 packets (about ⅔ cup) Instant Healthy Grain Original Cream of Wheat®, unsweetened

1 cup pomegranate or cranberry/raspberry juice

½ cup water

½ cup fresh or frozen raspberries

Sugar, to taste

Combine cereal, juice, water, and raspberries in a pot. Mash the raspberries with the back of a spoon if you don't want them to be visible. Bring to a boil, reduce to simmer, and cook for about 2 minutes until it reaches desired consistency.

PER SERVING: Calories 140; Total Fat 0.4g; Saturated Fat 0.1g; Trans Fat 0g; Cholesterol 10mg; Sodium 8mg; Carbohydrate 32.7g; Dietary Fiber 2.5g; Sugars 17.4g; Protein 2.1g; Vitamin A 13%; Vitamin C 13%; Calcium 7%; Iron 25%.

Quick Tip:

Cranberry juice contains quinic acid which reduces the amount of calcium in urine and helps to prevent kidney stones and urinary tract infections.

Roll-Out-the-Door Cheese Omelet

Carrots give this dish a delicately sweet taste and turns the egg whites a yolk-like color. Because the puree makes the eggs a little runny, it's best when it it's contained in this nifty roll-up, rather than on a plain old plate. Fast, easy, and handy—what more can you ask for?

3 minutes

MAKES 1 SERVING

Butter for pan

3 tablespoons liquid egg white or
   1 large egg

3 tablespoons Orange Puree (see Make-Ahead Recipe #2, p. 45) or baby food carrot puree

1 flour tortilla, ideally whole grain

1 slice 2% American cheese

Salt, to taste

Melt butter in a small nonstick skillet over medium heat. Pour egg into a mixing bowl and whisk in the puree until well incorporated. Add the beaten egg mixture to the skillet, allow to set briefly, and then, using a rubber spatula, lift edges of eggs as they cook, letting the uncooked part run underneath until omelet is completely set.

Slide the omelet onto the tortilla. Top with a slice of cheese, season with salt, and roll up. The cheese will melt under the hot eggs.

PER SERVING: Calories 214; Total Fat 9.6g; Saturated Fat 2.5g; Trans Fat 0g; Cholesterol 190mg; Sodium 661mg; Carbohydrate 25.4g; Dietary Fiber 14.9g; Sugars 3.4g; Protein 18.7g; Vitamin A 42%; Vitamin C 3%; Calcium 30%; Iron 4%.

Eggs

Eggs are power-houses! They contain vitamin D; lutein which protects your eyes; and high-quality protein which helps you to feel fuller longer and stay energized and maintain a healthy weight. The yolk contains choline, which is important for brain health. And contrary to popular belief, the cholesterol in eggs has virtually no effect on the cholesterol in your blood.

Strawberries

A serving of these sweet berries gives you as much vitamin C as an orange and is a great source of folic acid, fiber, potassium, and antioxidants. Strawberries keep your brain and heart healthy and help ward off cancer.

Strawberry Cheesecake English Muffins

No high-fructose corn syrup sneaking into this recipe! The real berries give this breakfast a classic cream cheese and jelly flavor without the heart-clogging fat. The ricotta adds a dose of calcium and protein. Here's another bonus: part-skim ricotta has more than twice the calcium and protein of cream cheese with only half the fat!

MAKES 1 SERVING

2 teaspoons reduced-fat cream cheese

2 teaspoons part-skim ricotta cheese

2 large strawberries, fresh or frozen, thawed

1 English muffin, ideally whole grain, split

Optional extra boost: **1 tablespoon chopped walnuts**

Combine cream cheese and ricotta on a plate. Mash strawberries into the cheese mixture with the back of a fork until they are fully incorporated into the cheese. Mix in nuts, if using. Spread evenly on toasted English muffin halves. Serve open-faced or closed.

PER SERVING: Calories 148; Total Fat 4g; Saturated Fat 1.9g; Trans Fat 0g; Cholesterol 12mg; Sodium 244mg; Carbohydrate 29.9g; Dietary Fiber 9g; Sugars 3.6g; Protein 7.3g; Vitamin A 3%; Vitamin C 40%; Calcium 11%; Iron 7%.

Banango Breakfast Popsicles

Emily and Samantha wanted to cook with me after dinner one evening. We rummaged through the kitchen and found some frozen mango and bananas, so we decided to make smoothies. We had some smoothie leftover in the blender, and rather than waste it, we froze it in cute popsicle molds. The girls could hardly wait until they were solid, so the next morning, I let them eat 'em for breakfast—after all, it's good-for-you fruit and yogurt, disguised as a treat!

MAKES 2 SERVINGS

1 cup frozen mango, no added syrup or sugar

1 cup low-fat banana or vanilla yogurt

1 ripe banana, peeled and chopped

¼ cup Orange Puree (see Make-Ahead Recipe #2, p. 45)

1 to 2 tablespoons sugar

2 Popsicle molds and sticks

Put all ingredients in a blender and puree on high (add a little more yogurt if needed to make a smooth consistency). Pour into popsicle molds, insert stick, and freeze for at least 30 minutes.

PER SERVING: Calories 210; Total Fat 0.6g; Saturated Fat 0.1g; Trans Fat 0g; Cholesterol 2mg; Sodium 64mg; Carbohydrate 49.8g; Dietary Fiber 4.1g; Sugars 35.7g; Protein 4.1g; Vitamin A 44%; Vitamin C 51%; Calcium 11%; Iron 1%.

Nutrition Burst

Yogurt

This calcium-rich food contains "friendly" bacteria (probiotics) that improve immune function and also protect against food poisoning.

Waffle Ice Cream Sandwiches

Swapping a sweet fruit and berry mixture for maple syrup is loads healthier for you and your family, but you'd never know it from looking at these waffles à la mode. You'll have to look quickly, though, as these never last long on the plate.

MAKES 2 SERVINGS

1 cup frozen mixed berries (such as blueberries, blackberries, strawberries and/or raspberries), unthawed, no added syrup or sugar

½ cup low-fat vanilla or berry yogurt

4 whole-grain waffles, toasted

Optional: 2 teaspoons honey or sugar

Fill bowl of food processor with frozen fruit and pulse several times to start the puree. Add yogurt and optional sugar or honey and puree on high until smooth, stopping if needed to scrape down the sides of the bowl and push contents to the bottom. The yogurt will be soft—spoon about ½ cup onto a warm waffle, top with another waffle, and serve immediately, or freeze yogurt mixture (without waffles) to use later (keeps in freezer for up to 3 months).

PER SERVING: Calories 232; Total Fat 6g; Saturated Fat 1.5g; Trans Fat 0g; Cholesterol 1mg; Sodium 425mg; Carbohydrate 39.8g; Dietary Fiber 5.5g; Sugars 12.1g; Protein 5.7g; Vitamin A 23%; Vitamin C 30%; Calcium 16%; Iron 22%.

Strawberry Short Shake

Thanks to my brother-in-law Ronny, I not only had a terrific taste-tester visiting for the holidays, but a clever recipe-namer! We all love strawberry shortcake, so why not put that flavor in a glass? I hung a mini waffle (the "cake" part) off the side of a tall glass and stuck in a straw for extra flair.

MAKES 2 SERVINGS

½ cup low-fat milk

¼ cup low-fat cottage cheese

¼ cup low-fat strawberry yogurt

8 strawberries (about ½ cup fresh or frozen), no added syrup or sweetener

Handful of ice, if not using frozen strawberries

2 whole-grain mini waffles, toasted

Optional: whipped cream and honey or sweetener, to taste

In a blender, combine all ingredients except the waffles. Blend until smooth. Pour into tall glasses. Make a small cut in each waffle and hang off the side of each glass. Serve with straws and top with a squirt of whipped cream, if desired. Add honey or sweetener to taste, if desired.

PER SERVING: Calories 102; Total Fat 2g; Saturated Fat 1g; Trans Fat 0g; Cholesterol 10mg; Sodium 198mg; Carbohydrate 15.1g; Dietary Fiber 1.2g; Sugars 8.4g; Protein 6.6g; Vitamin A 8%; Vitamin C 39%; Calcium 16%; Iron 5%.

Nutrition Burst

Calcium

Less than one-half of children and teens are getting enough calcium, according to the latest government statistics. Calcium is vital for developing bone mass, nearly all of which is built during childhood and adolescence. Being deficient can interfere with growth now and increase the risk of osteoporosis later in life.

Nutrition Burst

Chocolate

Delicious and good for you, cocoa is a natural disease-fighter—it's even more effective than red wine or tea. The flavonoids in one daily cup of cocoa may help drive heart disease away, according to researchers. Plus, chocolate has been shown to improve mood and brain function in young adults.

Hot Cocoa Breakfast Popsicles

Cocoa is practically a health food thanks to its high antioxidant content. I've kicked it up a nutritional notch with wheat germ, veggies, and milk, giving you a high-powered pop for breakfast or a snack.

MAKES ABOUT 6 SERVINGS

1 cup low-fat milk

4 tablespoons Orange Puree (see Make-
   Ahead Recipe #2, p. 45

3 tablespoons hot cocoa mix, sweetened

2 tablespoons wheat germ

Optional: handful of chocolate chips or
   mini marshmallows

6 Popsicle molds and sticks

In a blender, combine all ingredients except chocolate chips or marshmallows, if using. Blend until smooth. Drop a couple of chips or mini marshmallows into the bottom of each Popsicle mold, then pour in the cocoa mixture, insert stick, and freeze for at least 3 hours.

PER SERVING: Calories 52; Total Fat 1.2g; Saturated Fat 0.4g; Trans Fat 0g; Cholesterol 2mg; Sodium 68mg; Carbohydrate 8g; Dietary Fiber 0.8g; Sugars 4g; Protein 2.6g; Vitamin A 10%; Vitamin C 1%; Calcium 7%; Iron 2%.

Tropical Twist Breakfast Ice-Cream Cones

A wafer ice-cream cone has a mere 30 calories and no sugar, something you can't say about most kids' sugary breakfast cereals! Cones make a fun handheld "bowl" for this healthy and delicious morning treat. This recipe makes a soft-serve consistency, but you can make it harder by freezing it—just be sure to let it thaw a few minutes before eating.

MAKES 2 SERVINGS

½ cup frozen mango, no added syrup or sugar

½ cup frozen strawberries, no added syrup or sugar

1 banana, peeled and chopped (frozen or fresh)

½ cup low-fat milk

1 to 2 tablespoons honey or sugar

4 wafer ice-cream cones

Fill bowl of food processor with frozen fruit and pulse several times to start the puree. Add banana, milk, and sugar and puree on high until smooth, stopping if needed to scrape down the sides of the bowl and push contents to the bottom. Ice cream will be soft—fill cones to just below the top, cover with plastic wrap, and freeze to further harden (or fill cones and serve immediately).

PER SERVING: Calories 198; Total Fat 1.3g; Saturated Fat 0.6g; Trans Fat 0g; Cholesterol 2mg; Sodium 48mg; Carbohydrate 45.9g; Dietary Fiber 3.9g; Sugars 26.2g; Protein 3.8g; Vitamin A 11%; Vitamin C 69%; Calcium 10%; Iron 6%.

Elvis Breakfast Ice Cream

Sneaky Chef "breakfast ice cream" remains among the most popular recipes of my first book, and this "Elvis" version was inspired by the peanut butter, banana, and bacon sandwich named in honor of the King of Rock 'n' Roll. Bacon is optional, but I have to say, delicious!

MAKES 2 SERVINGS

2 frozen bananas (about 2 cups), chopped

¼ cup low-fat vanilla yogurt

1 tablespoon creamy peanut butter

1 to 2 tablespoons sugar

Optional: 2 tablespoons crumbled, cooked bacon

Put all ingredients (except bacon) in food processor and puree on high—hold on tight, the first few seconds will be a bit rough until the mixture smoothes out (add a little more yogurt if needed to make a smooth consistency). Serve in parfait glasses and top with crumbled bacon, if using. If you desire harder ice cream, freeze for at least 30 minutes.

PER SERVING: Calories 195; Total Fat 4g; Saturated Fat 0.8g; Trans Fat 0g; Cholesterol 0mg; Sodium 50mg; Carbohydrate 39.7g; Dietary Fiber 3.5g; Sugars 23.9g; Protein 3.8g; Vitamin A 3%; Vitamin C 20%; Calcium 3%; Iron 3%.

Hot Apple Pie Parfait

5 minutes

Nothing beats the aroma of apples sautéing in butter and cinnamon on an early school morning. This dish will lure even the grumpiest kid— or hubby—out of bed with a smile.

MAKES 2 PARFAITS

2 teaspoons unsalted butter

1 large apple, cored, and thinly sliced, ideally unpeeled or 1 packet of presliced apples, such as Mott's®

2 teaspoons brown sugar

Pinch of cinnamon or apple pie spice

½ cup low-fat granola

2 tablespoons ground flaxseed and/or wheat germ

½ cup low-fat vanilla yogurt

Add butter to saucepan and melt over medium heat. Mix in the apple slices, brown sugar, and cinnamon or spice, sautéing for about 5 minutes. Add a tablespoon of water to pan if apple mixture gets too dry.

In parfait or serving glasses, layer granola/flax/wheat germ, yogurt, and apples as desired, and serve.

PER SERVING: Calories 268; Total Fat 7.8g; Saturated Fat 3g; Trans Fat 0g; Cholesterol 11mg; Sodium 78mg; Carbohydrate 43.3g; Dietary Fiber 6.3g; Sugars 21.5g; Protein 7.2g; Vitamin A 11%; Vitamin C 7%; Calcium 9%; Iron 11%.

LUNCH
RECIPES

BBQ Chicken Mac 'n' Cheese

12 minutes

Sammy never liked taking chicken to school for lunch, but when I put this dish in her thermos (albeit a gluten-free version), she came home and told me

I had given her two of her favorite foods in one! I don't know who was happier—Sammy or her mother who had managed to sneak in some more brain-boosting protein into her daughter's day! Maybe that's why she aced the math test!

MAKES 4 SERVINGS

1 (6-ounce) box macaroni and cheese, ideally whole grain

¼ cup low-fat milk

2 tablespoons BBQ sauce

6 tablespoons White or Orange Puree (see Make-Ahead Recipe #4, p. 51 or Make-Ahead Recipe #2, p. 45) or baby food carrot or sweet potato puree

½ cup cooked chicken, diced

Boil macaroni according to package directions and drain. Combine milk, BBQ sauce, and puree in pot and return to simmer, stirring until well combined. Add in chicken, warm through, and serve.

PER SERVING: Calories 255; Total Fat 3.2g; Saturated Fat 1.6g; Trans Fat 0g; Cholesterol 27mg; Sodium 656mg; Carbohydrate 42.8g; Dietary Fiber 4.2g; Sugars 8.4g; Protein 13.8g; Vitamin A 1%; Vitamin C 8%; Calcium 10%; Iron 8%.

{ Sneaky shortcut }

Store your everyday dishes and glassware near the dishwasher, and your spices and cooking items next to the stove.

Presto Pizza Mac 'n' Cheese

12 minutes

Hard to believe kids could ever tire of boxed mac 'n' cheese, but this pizza version is a nice variation on the familiar and an opportunity to sneak in even more veggies. The tomato paste isn't just one of the ultimate ready-made healthy purees, it also lends an authentic pizza flavor to the recipe.

MAKES 3 SERVINGS

1 (6-ounce) box macaroni and cheese, ideally whole grain

¼ cup low-fat milk

2 tablespoons tomato paste

3 tablespoons Orange Puree (see Make-Ahead Recipe #2, p. 45) or baby food carrot or sweet potato puree

Optional toppings: handful of diced low-fat pepperoni (turkey, soy, or other), sliced mushrooms, olives, or other favorite pizza "toppings"

Boil macaroni according to package directions and drain. Combine milk, tomato paste, and puree in pot and return to simmer, stirring until well combined. Add in pepperoni and/or other toppings, if using, and serve.

PER SERVING: Calories 289; Total Fat 3.8g; Saturated Fat 2.2g; Trans Fat 0g; Cholesterol 16mg; Sodium 622mg; Carbohydrate 54.1g; Dietary Fiber 5.7g; Sugars 7.5g; Protein 9.7g; Vitamin A 17%; Vitamin C 5%; Calcium 13%; Iron 11%.

Quick Tip:

In some brands, yellow macaroni and cheese contains yellow food dye, whereas the white version does not.

Parmesan Chicken Fries

Why didn't anyone tell me that bread crumbs can stick to meat just fine with-out the time-consuming flour/egg/breadcrumb 3-step process? News flash! Raw skinless chicken is very sticky and holds this whole-grain breading quite well! No need for frying here; I used my "faux fry" method of high heat baking, using a generous coating of good-quality cooking spray oil to give these fries a nice crisp finish. A good pair of kitchen scissors is your best friend here for cutting the chicken into fry-shaped sticks.

MAKES 4 SERVINGS

2 tablespoons ground flaxseed

2 tablespoons wheat germ

1 cup breadcrumbs, ideally whole grain

12 ounces uncooked boneless, skinless, thinly sliced chicken breasts

Cooking spray oil

Dip:

½ cup store-bought marinara sauce

¼ cup Orange Puree (see Make-Ahead Recipe #2, p. 45) or baby food carrot or sweet potato puree

Preheat oven to 425 degrees and generously coat baking sheet with cooking spray oil.

Cut tenders into French fry–shaped strips, easily done using kitchen scissors. Combine flax, wheat germ, and bread-crumbs in zip-top plastic bag, seal, and shake to mix. Add chicken strips, seal, and shake to coat chicken evenly. Remove chicken pieces and place on prepared bak-ing sheet. Generously coat top of chicken with more cooking spray and bake for 12 to 14 minutes or until browned and cooked through.

Combine marinara sauce with puree and serve as dip alongside the chicken fries.

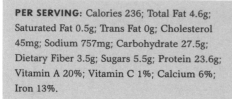

PER SERVING: Calories 236; Total Fat 4.6g; Saturated Fat 0.5g; Trans Fat 0g; Cholesterol 45mg; Sodium 757mg; Carbohydrate 27.5g; Dietary Fiber 3.5g; Sugars 5.5g; Protein 23.6g; Vitamin A 20%; Vitamin C 1%; Calcium 6%; Iron 13%.

{ *Sneaky shortcut* }

Oven frying isn't only healthier for you, it's faster, too! Just spray one baking sheet with oil and jack the oven up to 400 degrees for a good, crisp oven-fried finish.

40-Second Soft Tacos

-1 minute

This is my family's "go-to" meal when we don't want to really cook, and don't want to go out. They're so fast to put together, you can't even beat the speed of these with a frozen version! The secret to a soft taco is to microwave the tortilla in wet paper towels. Plus, these tacos are nutritional powerhouses—the vitamin C in the tomato paste helps our bodies absorb the iron in the beans.

MAKES 4 TACOS (2 SERVINGS)

6 tablespoons canned refried beans, no lard

2 tablespoons tomato paste

2 tablespoons wheat germ or ground flaxseed

Pinch of salt

½ cup shredded, reduced-fat Mexican cheese

4 (6-inch round) corn or flour tortillas, ideally whole grain

Optional toppings: **dash of taco seasoning, shredded lettuce, salsa, and/or plain Greek yogurt**

In a mixing bowl, combine the refried beans, tomato paste, and wheat germ or flax. Lay a few wet paper towels on the microwave turntable, place 2 of the tortillas on the paper towels, and top each tortilla with about 2 tablespoons of the bean mixture. Top each with about 2 tablespoons cheese and a pinch of salt. Leave open-faced and microwave on high for 40 seconds. Remove tacos from microwave, add optional toppings, fold in half and serve warm. Repeat with remaining 2 tacos.

PER SERVING: Calories 289; Total Fat 10.2g; Saturated Fat 3.5g; Trans Fat 0g; Cholesterol 15mg; Sodium 606mg; Carbohydrate 39.1g; Dietary Fiber 8.8g; Sugars 4.5g; Protein 14.8g; Vitamin A 13%; Vitamin C 5%; Calcium 24%; Iron 10%.

Chicken Parm Soup

10 minutes

Packaged, flavored brown rice does twice the work for you. It provides quick, whole grains and eliminates the need for you to add any other salt or spices to the soup. With these pantry and refrigerated staples on hand, you can whip up a fresh, homemade soup in less than 10 minutes.

MAKES 4 SERVINGS

1 cup uncooked Uncle Ben's Ready Rice®, Chicken Flavored Whole Grain Brown Rice

3 cups chicken broth, reduced sodium

3 tablespoons grated Parmesan cheese

½ cup White Puree (See Make-Ahead Recipe #4, p. 51) or butternut squash puree (frozen or baby food squash puree)

¼ cup tomato paste

6 ounces (about 1 cup) cooked chicken, diced or shredded

Optional extra boost: fresh sliced carrots and celery

Place all ingredients in a soup pot and bring to a boil over medium high heat. Reduce to simmer for about 5 to 10 minutes (or until carrots are tender, if using), stirring occasionally.

Remove soup from heat and ladle soup into individual bowls.

PER SERVING: Calories 214; Total Fat 3.7g; Saturated Fat 1g; Trans Fat 0g; Cholesterol 38mg; Sodium 496mg; Carbohydrate 25.9g; Dietary Fiber 2.6g; Sugars 2.8g; Protein 19.5g; Vitamin A 6%; Vitamin C 15%; Calcium 5%; Iron 8%.

Quick Tip:

Research has shown that the vitamin C in vegetables like cauliflower can help reduce the wheezing in children suffering from asthma.

Rapid Ravioli Soup

This recipe adds a healthy homemade touch to kids' favorite canned ravioli. The nonfat dry milk not only gives it a nice boost of calcium and protein, but also smooths out the red sauce. Best yet? This delicious, creamy soup takes only 5 minutes.

MAKES 4 SERVINGS

¼ cup Orange Puree (see Make-Ahead Recipe #2, p. 45) or baby food carrot or sweet potato puree

1 cup vegetable broth, reduced sodium

1 (15-ounce) can ravioli in tomato sauce

2 tablespoons nonfat dry milk

Optional extra boost: fresh chopped basil and fresh sliced carrots

Place all ingredients in a soup pot and bring to a boil over medium high heat. Reduce to simmer for about 2 minutes (or until carrots are tender, if using), stirring occasionally.

Remove soup from heat and ladle soup into individual bowls.

PER SERVING: Calories 115; Total Fat 1.8g; Saturated Fat 0.8g; Trans Fat 0g; Cholesterol 3mg; Sodium 429mg; Carbohydrate 19.9g; Dietary Fiber 2g; Sugars 7.5g; Protein 4.6g; Vitamin A 18%; Vitamin C 3%; Calcium 10%; Iron 6%.

Valentine's Soup

*Kids (even big kids) will eat almost any soup with chopped-up hot dogs in it!
I've even found kids who don't normally eat tomato soup love this soup
not only for its smoky flavor, but for its deep red, Valentine color.
I especially love the fact that the vitamin C–rich tomatoes help us
absorb the iron from the white beans.*

10 minutes

MAKES 4 SERVINGS

3 cups tomato soup, ideally reduced
sodium

½ cup cooked or canned beets

6 tablespoons White Bean Puree (see
Make-Ahead Recipe #5, p. 54) or ½ cup
canned white beans, rinsed and drained

3 hot dogs, ideally nitrate-free, chopped

Place all ingredients except hot dogs in a blender and puree on high until smooth. Pour into a soup pot, add hot dogs, and bring to a boil over medium high heat. Reduce to simmer for about 5 to 10 minutes, stirring occasionally.

Remove soup from heat and ladle soup into individual bowls.

PER SERVING: Calories 176; Total Fat 3.2g; Saturated Fat 1.5g; Trans Fat 0g; Cholesterol 19mg; Sodium 626mg; Carbohydrate 28.9g; Dietary Fiber 3.8g; Sugars 12.9g; Protein 8.5g; Vitamin A 15%; Vitamin C 46%; Calcium 8%; Iron 11%.

PARMESAN CHICKEN FRIES *Sneaky ingredients:* Flaxseed, wheat germ, carrots, sweet potatoes (p. 115)
VALENTINE'S SOUP *Sneaky ingredients:* Tomatoes, beets, white beans (p. 120)

CHEESY CHICKEN LUNCHBOX MUFFINS *Sneaky ingredients:* Carrots, sweet potatoes (p. 133)
TOO-GOOD-TO-BE-TRUE TAQUITOS *Sneaky ingredients:* Flaxseed, spinach, broccoli, peas (p. 136)

BBQ CHICKEN MAC 'N' CHEESE *Sneaky ingredients (2 versions):* Cauliflower and zucchini or carrots and sweet potatoes (p. 113)

RIDICULOUSLY EASY RAVIOLI LASAGNA *Sneaky ingredients:* Cauliflower, zucchini, carrots (p. 192)

CHICKEN PARM POPS *Sneaky ingredients:* Carrots, sweet potatoes (p. 155)

PRESTO PIZZA MAC 'N' CHEESE *Sneaky ingredients:* Carrots, sweet potatoes, tomatoes (p. 114)

SMOKY JOE SLIDERS *Sneaky ingredients:* Refried beans, blueberries, spinach, tomatoes, whole grains (p. 170)

CRISPY COCONUT-CRUSTED CHICKEN *Sneaky ingredients:* Butternut squash, oat bran (p. 160)
SWIFT SHRIMP TERIYAKI KEBOBS *Sneaky ingredients:* Cauliflower, zucchini (p. 166)

SWIFT SPAGHETTI & MEATBALL PIZZA *Sneaky ingredients (2 versions):* Whole grains; cauliflower and zucchini or carrots and sweet potatoes (p. 186)

EASY-TO-DO BBQ CHICKEN PIZZA *Sneaky ingredients (2 versions):* Flaxseed, whole grains; spinach, broccoli, peas or cauliflower and zucchini (p. 149)

California Roll Bowl

The brilliance of this is it's all the loveable taste of a California roll without the time-consuming detail of rolling sticky rice into neat sushi rolls. This recipe also allows you to use whole grain rice since you don't have to worry about it sticking together.

MAKES 4 SERVINGS

8 crab sticks, "imitation crab" okay

1 ripe avocado

¼ cup Green Puree (see Make-Ahead Recipe #3, p. 48)

1 tablespoon freshly squeezed lemon juice

2 cups cooked brown rice or whole-grain white rice (such as Uncle Ben's®)

1 cup seedless cucumber, peeled and chopped

Optional garnish: 2 tablespoons sesame seeds and 2 large sheets "Nori" seaweed

Cut crab sticks and seaweed, if using, into about one-inch pieces. This is easily done using kitchen scissors. Set aside.

In a large serving bowl, mash the avocado with the puree and lemon juice. Mix in the rice, cucumber, crab, and seaweed and sesame seeds, if using, and serve at room temperature.

PER SERVING: Calories 226; Total Fat 8.1g; Saturated Fat 1.1g; Trans Fat 0g; Cholesterol 50mg; Sodium 413mg; Carbohydrate 29.3g; Dietary Fiber 5.4g; Sugars 2.4g; Protein 11.1g; Vitamin A 4%; Vitamin C 14%; Calcium 4%; Iron 7%.

Nutrition Burst

Avocado

This fruit is named by the *Guinness Book of World Records* **as** the world's most nutritious. The avocado is virtually the only fruit that has monounsaturated fat (the good fat), which can help boost HDL (good cholesterol) and lower LDL (bad cholesterol). This wonderful "good fat" is especially good for baby's brains and physical development. Avocados also have a higher fiber content than any other fruit with 30 percent of your daily recommended amount in a single cup.

Pita Triangles with Cheesy Pizza Dip

Don't let the word "dip" fool you, this veggie-packed, high-protein fun dish is a nutritionally sound minimeal!

MAKES 4 SERVINGS

4 large "Greek-style" pocketless pitas or "Naan," ideally whole grain

2 cups store-bought pizza sauce

½ cup White Puree (see Make-Ahead Recipe #4, p. 51) or baby food carrot or sweet potato puree

2 tablespoons grated Parmesan cheese

Optional: ¼ teaspoon dried oregano and/or basil

Cut pita or Naan bread into strips or triangles, easily done with kitchen scissors.

Mix remaining ingredients, including optional oregano or basil if using, in a microwave-safe bowl. Cover the top of the bowl with a wet paper towel and microwave on high for 1 minute or until heated through. Serve bread triangles with warm pizza dip.

PER SERVING: Calories 318; Total Fat 3.8g; Saturated Fat 0.4g; Trans Fat 0g; Cholesterol 2mg; Sodium 354mg; Carbohydrate 57.6g; Dietary Fiber 8.6g; Sugars 2.8g; Protein 14.5g; Vitamin A 0%; Vitamin C 10%; Calcium 5%; Iron 15%.

Hushh Puppy Muffins

14 minutes

Hush puppies are a deep-fried, cornmeal-based Southern specialty, tradition-ally served alongside fish. Folklore says they got their name from Confeder-ate soldiers and hunters who would give them to their dogs to "hush" them. Here's a fun way to get all the taste and almost none of the fat of traditional hush puppies. Your kids won't notice the switcheroo, but they'll be howling for more!

MAKES 3 DOZEN

1 large egg

½ cup White Puree (See Make-Ahead Recipe #4, p. 51) or baby food sweet potato puree

¼ cup low-fat buttermilk

2 tablespoons canola oil

¼ cup fresh or frozen chopped onion

1 (approximately 6½-ounce) can of lump or fancy white crabmeat

¼ cup dry oat bran

1 (approximately 8½-ounce) box of corn muffin mix

PER SERVING (2 MUFFINS): Calories 60; Total Fat 2g; Saturated Fat 0.2g; Trans Fat 0g; Cholesterol 9mg; Sodium 134mg; Carbohydrate 7.9g; Dietary Fiber 1.1g; Sugars 1.3g; Protein 2.9g; Vitamin A 0%; Vitamin C 2%; Calcium 1%; Iron 2%.

Preheat oven to 400 degrees and grease or spray mini muffin tins with oil.

In a large bowl, whisk together the egg, puree, buttermilk, and oil. Stir in the onion, crabmeat, oat bran, and corn muffin mix, mixing until the dry ingredients are just in-corporated into the wet.

Scoop mixture evenly into prepared muf-fin tins. Bake 12 to 14 minutes, or until a tooth-pick inserted in the center comes out clean.

{ Sneaky shortcut }

Save time (and money) on doing your nails by using thick, lined rubber gloves when you do the dishes.

Cheesy Chicken Lunchbox Muffins

I used to walk right by the wonton wrappers in the produce section of my market, never having appreciated what a simple and versatile ingredient they are. But one day when all attempts to find the perfect, low-fat, pliable crust failed, I gave wonton wrappers a whirl, and boy, am I glad I did. They provide a ready-made pre-cut piece of dough with very few ingredients and no fat and work beautifully as a thin but sturdy crust for mini quiches and this savory lunchbox muffin.

20 minutes

MAKES 6 MUFFINS

1 large egg

¼ cup reduced-fat cream cheese

½ teaspoon onion powder

½ teaspoon salt

½ cup Orange Puree (see Make-Ahead Recipe #2, p. 45) or baby food carrot or sweet potato puree

1 cup cooked chicken, diced

6 wonton wrappers

½ cup shredded, reduced-fat cheddar cheese

PER SERVING: Calories 147; Total Fat 2.5g; Saturated Fat 1.5g; Trans Fat 0g; Cholesterol 40mg; Sodium 387mg; Carbohydrate 7.8g; Dietary Fiber 0.4g; Sugars 1.4g; Protein 16.9g; Vitamin A 23%; Vitamin C 1%; Calcium 14%; Iron 8%.

Preheat oven 400 degrees and grease or spray muffin tins with oil.

In a mixing bowl, whisk together the egg, cream cheese, onion powder, salt, and Orange Puree. Mix in the chicken. Press one wonton wrapper into each muffin tin so that it covers the bottom and comes up the sides of each muffin tin. Pour ¼ cup of mixture into each tin, top with about one tablespoon of shredded cheese each, and bake for 20 minutes or until edges of wonton are golden, cheese is melted, and filling is firmly set. Serve warm or cold in the lunch box.

Chocolate Banana Cream Pie Sneak-Wich

0 minutes

This sandwich boasts the classic French combination of Nutella® and bananas. The cream cheese and white bean puree gives it a healthy twist and balances the sweetness of the chocolate and bananas. If you have time, take it over the top by dipping it in egg batter and pan frying it for a French toast sandwich! Ooh la la!

MAKES 1 SANDWICH

1 tablespoon hazelnut-chocolate spread, such as Nutella®

1 tablespoon reduced-fat cream cheese

2 teaspoons White Bean Puree (See Make-Ahead Recipe #4, p. 54)

1 teaspoon ground flaxseed

2 slices whole-grain bread

½ banana, sliced

In a mixing bowl, combine hazelnut-chocolate spread, cream cheese, puree, and flax. Spread evenly over each slice of bread, top with sliced banana, then close, cut in half, and serve.

PER SERVING: Calories 395; Total Fat 9.3g; Saturated Fat 1.8g; Trans Fat 0g; Cholesterol 13mg; Sodium 369mg; Carbohydrate 66.4g; Dietary Fiber 10g; Sugars 29.5g; Protein 14.2g; Vitamin A 5%; Vitamin C 8%; Calcium 19%; Iron 18%.

Turkey Club Sub

2 minutes

Kids seem to love anything served up in a hot dog bun, and there are finally some soft whole-grain ones in the market. Like a club sandwich with the bacon, turkey, lettuce, and tomato, this sub boasts hidden veggie power and cuts the fat without losing flavor. It's quick and easy for the lunchbox, especially if you keep a stash of cooked turkey bacon on hand in the fridge.

MAKES 1 SANDWICH

1 tablespoon ketchup

1 tablespoon Orange Puree (see Make-Ahead Recipe #2, p. 45) or baby food carrot or sweet potato puree

1 hot dog bun, ideally whole grain or white whole wheat

2 slices turkey bacon, cooked

2 deli slices smoked turkey

Optional extra boost: tomato slices, lettuce, sliced pickle

In a mixing bowl, combine ketchup and puree. Spread ketchup mixture on bun, then add bacon, turkey, and any optional extras.

PER SERVING: Calories 211; Total Fat 3.7g; Saturated Fat 0.5g; Trans Fat 0g; Cholesterol 35mg; Sodium 902mg; Carbohydrate 28.5g; Dietary Fiber 2.3g; Sugars 8g; Protein 17.1g; Vitamin A 15%; Vitamin C 1%; Calcium 4%; Iron 6%.

Quick Tip:

Take a walk in the sunshine for double benefits. Exercise, plus 10 minutes of exposure to the sun per day, can produce 10,000 IUs of bone-strengthening and immune-boosting vitamin D.

Too-Good-to-Be-True Taquitos

A taquito is a small rolled burrito that's usually deep-fried. I make my good-for-you version a few batches at a time and freeze them. When it's time to load up the lunchboxes, I simply thaw them in the microwave.

MAKES 8 TAQUITOS (4 SERVINGS)

4 ounces cooked chicken, turkey, or ham

2 tablespoons ground flaxseed

¼ cup Green Puree (see Make-Ahead Recipe #3, p. 48) or baby food mixed green vegetable puree

¼ cup tomato paste

1 to 2 tablespoons taco seasoning mix (packaged) or Make-Ahead "Instant" Taco Seasoning Recipe, p. 76

8 (6-inch round) corn tortillas (white or yellow)

½ cup shredded, reduced-fat Mexican or cheddar cheese

Toothpicks

Preheat oven to 400 degrees and spray a baking sheet with oil.

Cut chicken, turkey, or ham into thin strips, easily done using kitchen scissors. Set aside.

In a mixing bowl, combine the flax, puree, tomato paste, and seasoning.

Wrap tortillas in damp paper towels and microwave on high for 30 seconds to one minute to make soft and pliable (you may want to do a few tortillas at a time so they don't get stiff again).

Remove paper towels and lay soft tortillas out on the baking sheet. Spread each with about one tablespoon of the tomato mixture, top with about ½ ounce of chicken, turkey, or ham, and one tablespoon of cheese. Roll tightly and place seam-side down on the baking sheet (secure with a toothpick, if necessary). Spray the tops of the taquitos with more oil and bake for 10 minutes or until lightly browned. Remove toothpicks and serve warm, or allow to cool and freeze for up to 3 months (simply pop the taquito in microwave).

PER SERVING: Calories 119; Total Fat 3.1g; Saturated Fat 0.9g; Trans Fat 0g; Cholesterol 17mg; Sodium 224mg; Carbohydrate 15.4g; Dietary Fiber 2.3g; Sugars 1.4g; Protein 8g; Vitamin A 8%; Vitamin C 6%; Calcium 11%; Iron 6%.

Lemony Tuna Pita Pocket

Hummus is available everywhere nowadays; you can even pick some up at the local convenience store. Lemon-flavored hummus adds a double boost of flavor and nutrition to tuna salad, and offers a "good fat" alternative to traditional mayonnaise. Once your family tries this version, they may never go back to boring and bland tuna salad again!

MAKES 2 SERVINGS

1 (6-ounce) can "chunk light" tuna, packed in water, drained

2 tablespoons store-bought classic or lemon-flavored hummus

4 mini pita pockets or 2 large pita pockets, ideally whole grain

Optional extra boost: handful each, diced tomatoes, cucumbers, and/or carrots

Combine the tuna and hummus in a bowl, mashing with the back of a fork. Mix in any optional ingredients, if using. Spoon tuna mixture into pita pockets and serve.

PER SERVING: Calories 255; Total Fat 3.2g; Saturated Fat 0g; Trans Fat 0g; Cholesterol 45mg; Sodium 755mg; Carbohydrate 30.5g; Dietary Fiber 5.5g; Sugars 2g; Protein 27g; Vitamin A 0%; Vitamin C 0%; Calcium 6%; Iron 12%.

Quick Tip:

"Chunk light" tuna often packs less harmful mercury than "chunk white" tuna.

Quick Tip:

Put the salt-shaker down! For every 2,300 milligrams of sodium you take in, you lose about 40 milligrams of calcium, weakening bones over time, dietitians say. Some fast fixes: pass on sodium-heavy processed foods and opt for frozen over canned veggies.

Nutrition Burst

Chickpeas

Also known as garbanzo beans, chickpeas are high in fiber, folate, tryptophan, magnesium, and iron, protecting your heart and giving you an energy boost. When they're paired with simple carbs, they help keep your blood sugar steady.

Meatball Calzone

This recipe satisfies a yearning for an old-fashioned calzone from the Italian restaurant, but is sneakily slimmed down. I swapped sandwich thin rolls for the pizza dough, which allows you to crimp the edges to seal in our meatball and cheesy goodness, while getting in a good dose of whole grains and hidden veggies and beans.

MAKES 2 SANDWICHES

½ cup store-bought marinara sauce

½ cup White or Orange Puree (see Make-Ahead Recipe #4, p. 51 or Make-Ahead Recipe #2, p. 48) or baby food carrot puree

4 cooked meatballs (frozen, prepared, or homemade), sliced in half

6 tablespoons shredded, reduced-fat mozzarella, divided

2 whole-grain flat breads, such as Arnold® "Sandwich Thin" or Pepperidge Farm® "Deli Flats"

Preheat oven to 400 degrees and line a baking sheet with foil.

In a mixing bowl, combine the marinara sauce and puree. Open flat breads and lay each half on the baking sheet. Spread about 1 tablespoon of marinara mixture on each half. Lay 4 meatball halves on the bottom 2 halves of the flat breads, leaving the other 2 halves with just sauce (these will be the tops). Sprinkle about 2 tablespoons of cheese over the meatballs, placing some of the cheese along the edges of the bread (this will hold the sandwiches together when it melts). Top each meatball half with a top and press gently together, crimping the edges closed with your fingers. Top each sandwich with about 1 more tablespoon of cheese in the center, then spray oil over all the sandwiches.

Bake for about 10 minutes or until the cheese on top is melted and bread is golden. Serve with remaining marinara sauce mixture, warmed.

PER SERVING: Calories 349; Total Fat 16.1g; Saturated Fat 5.8g; Trans Fat 0g; Cholesterol 70mg; Sodium 944mg; Carbohydrate 32.9g; Dietary Fiber 7.7g; Sugars 9.6g; Protein 24.8g; Vitamin A 21%; Vitamin C 21%; Calcium 29%; Iron 18%.

Quick Quinoa Bean Burrito

Quinoa is an ancient grain that is growing in popularity. It cooks faster than most other whole grains, in about 12 minutes. Move over mushy rice, this grain gives a great "pop" in your mouth. Plus, it's the only grain that makes a complete plant protein on its own. When you wrap quinoa with all the Mexican burrito fixins', no one will even notice the rice is missing. These burritos can be made a day ahead and refrigerated. Simply pop the wrapped burrito in the microwave for one minute before eating.

13 minutes

MAKES 2 SERVINGS

¼ cup quinoa

½ cup refried beans, no lard

1 to 2 teaspoons taco seasoning mix (packaged) or Make-Ahead "Instant" Taco Seasoning Recipe, p. 76

¼ cup White Puree (See Make-Ahead Recipe #4, p. 51 or butternut squash puree (frozen or baby food squash puree)

2 large flour tortillas, ideally whole grain

¼ cup shredded, reduced-fat Mexican blend or cheddar cheese

Optional toppings: chopped tomatoes and/or black olives, salsa, reduced-fat sour cream or plain Greek yogurt, chopped green onions

Cook quinoa according to package directions.

In a mixing bowl, combine refried beans, seasoning mix, and White Puree. Spoon about ¼ cup of the refried bean mixture and ¼ cup of the cooked quinoa onto the bottom third of each tortilla. Top with about 2 tablespoons of cheese and any or all of the optional toppings. Fold the bottom quarter of each tortilla up and over the filling, fold both sides toward the middle, and roll into sealed packets. Tightly wrap the packets in damp paper towels or parchment paper to secure. Microwave on high for 1 minute or until warmed through.

PER SERVING: Calories 356; Total Fat 7.2g; Saturated Fat 1.8g; Trans Fat 0g; Cholesterol 10mg; Sodium 600mg; Carbohydrate 61.3g; Dietary Fiber 7.3g; Sugars 1.8g; Protein 16.7g; Vitamin A 6%; Vitamin C 11%; Calcium 30%; Iron 31%.

No-Bake Peanut Butter Bar

Because my kids are always asking for protein bars, I wanted to come up with a simpler, homemade, less processed version. I was so excited to come up with a delicious, easy-to-make, "mini-meal-replacement" bar. This one requires no baking, so it is a speedy staple for peanut-friendly houses or schools. These are great as an after-school or after-sports snack. My husband eats them frozen, but I prefer mine slightly thawed so I can gobble it up even quicker!

MAKES ABOUT 12 BARS

1 cup Orange Puree (see Make-Ahead Recipe #2, p. 45) or baby food carrot puree

½ cup creamy peanut butter

2 tablespoons all-fruit jam

¾ cup nonfat dry milk powder

1 cup ground flaxseed

2 cups crispy rice cereal, ideally brown rice

¼ cup sugar, ideally raw sugar

Line an 8-inch or 9-inch square baking pan with foil, letting the foil extend over edges of pan. Spray with oil.

In a mixing bowl, combine puree and peanut butter, then stir in jam, milk powder, flax, and rice cereal. Pat into prepared pan, and sprinkle sugar evenly over the top. Freeze for at least one hour. Lift out foil and cut into approximately 12 rectangular bars, place in individual sealed plastic bags, or in a plastic container with wax paper between layers, and keep frozen for up to 3 months.

PER SERVING. Calories 176, Total Fat 8.4g, Saturated Fat 1g; Trans Fat 0g; Cholesterol 0mg; Sodium 18mg; Carbohydrate 20.3g; Dietary Fiber 3.7g; Sugars 10.5g; Protein 7.4g; Vitamin A 17%; Vitamin C 1%; Calcium 9%; Iron 4%.

Nutrition Burst

Peanut Butter

Peanuts aren't actually nuts—they're legumes, like beans and lentils. They're the enemy of high cholesterol and the antidote for blood sugar spikes. A serving of peanut butter has more protein than a large egg. And you'd never guess it, but peanut butter contains the nutrient resveratrol, which is the life-prolonging compound also found in red wine and grapes.

DINNER RECIPES

Oops the Wontons Fell Apart Soup

As the title suggests, this is an easy, messy solution to homemade wontons that invariably fall apart after the first bite anyway. Ginger, soy, and garlic instantly transform chicken broth into something entirely new.

8 minutes

MAKES 4 SERVINGS

2 tablespoons pomegranate juice

¼ cup Green Puree (see Make-Ahead Recipe #3, p. 48) or baby food mixed green vegetable puree

3 tablespoons reduced-sodium soy sauce

2 teaspoons grated fresh ginger or
½ teaspoon ground ginger

2 teaspoons minced fresh garlic or
½ teaspoon garlic powder

½ pound lean ground beef and/or pork

5 cups chicken broth, reduced sodium

12 wonton wrappers, cut in half diagonally

Optional garnish: ½ cup sliced scallions

In a mixing bowl, whisk together the pomegranate juice, puree, half of the soy sauce, half the ginger, and half the garlic (reserve the other half of these ingredients to add to the broth later). Mix in the meat.

Heat soup pot over medium. Add meat mixture, stirring to break it up, and cook for about 3 minutes until the meat is no longer red. Stir in the broth, remaining garlic, ginger, soy sauce, and wonton wrappers. Bring to a boil, and then reduce heat to low and simmer for 5 minutes.

Ladle into soup bowls and garnish with scallions, if using.

Quick Tip:

Ginger beats drugs for treating motion sickness and nausea.

PER SERVING: Calories 274; Total Fat 4.1g; Saturated Fat 1.5g; Trans Fat 0g; Cholesterol 32mg; Sodium 663mg; Carbohydrate 19.8g; Dietary Fiber 0.5g; Sugars 1.5g; Protein 18.3g; Vitamin A 2%; Vitamin C 5%; Calcium 1%; Iron 11%.

Miso Noodle Bowl

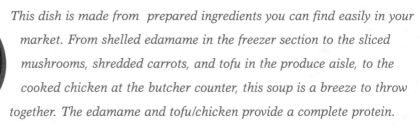

This dish is made from prepared ingredients you can find easily in your market. From shelled edamame in the freezer section to the sliced mushrooms, shredded carrots, and tofu in the produce aisle, to the cooked chicken at the butcher counter, this soup is a breeze to throw together. The edamame and tofu/chicken provide a complete protein. You can even add seaweed (a great source of iodine) if your kids are feeling adventurous. Just be careful not to boil miso because boiling kills some of the healthful enzymes.

MAKES 6–8 SERVINGS

6 ounces buckwheat (Soba) noodles or whole grain Udon noodles

8 cups water

1 cup shelled edamame, fresh or frozen

½ cup Orange Puree (see Make-Ahead Recipe #2, p. 45) or baby food sweet potato puree

1 cup cooked chicken, shredded and/or 1 cup cubed tofu

6 (approximately 3-ounce packets) instant miso soup mix

Optional extra boosts: ½ cup each, shredded carrots, sliced fresh mushrooms, scallions, and/or baby spinach leaves

Cook noodles according to package directions. Drain and set aside.

In a large soup pot, add water, edamame, any optional veggies (except scallions, if using—they go in at end), puree, and chicken and/or tofu, and bring to a boil. Reduce heat to simmer for about 5 minutes, then stir in the miso.

Divide noodles among large soup bowls and ladle soup on top. Garnish with scallions, if using, and serve hot.

PER SERVING: Calories 154; Total Fat 3.6g; Saturated Fat 0.3g; Trans Fat 0g; Cholesterol 0mg; Sodium 712mg; Carbohydrate 20.6g; Dietary Fiber 2.1g; Sugars 1.2g; Protein 9.8g; Vitamin A 13%; Vitamin C 5%; Calcium 14%; Iron 19%.

Easy-to-Do BBQ Chicken Pizza

Not only is this a great way to serve a handheld meal for families on the go, but it's a cinch to make. I keep cooked chicken breasts in my freezer at all times so I can throw this together faster than it takes to dial take-out.

15 minutes

MAKES 6 SERVINGS

½ cup store-bought BBQ sauce

⅓ cup White or Green Puree (see Make-Ahead Recipe #4, p. 51 or Make-Ahead Recipe #3, p. 48) or baby food mixed vegetable puree

2 tablespoons ground flaxseed

1 large (about 12-inch) store-bought pizza crust, ideally whole grain (such as Boboli® whole grain)

2 cups rotisserie or cooked chicken, cubed

1½ cups shredded, reduced-fat cheddar cheese

Optional extra boost: one small red onion and bell pepper, thinly sliced

Preheat oven to 450 degrees and preheat a pizza stone, if using, or spray a baking sheet with oil.

In a mixing bowl, combine BBQ sauce, puree, and flax. Spread half of the sauce mixture (about ½ cup) on the pizza crust. Add cubed chicken to the remaining sauce and toss to coat.

Sprinkle chicken, cheese, and optional onions and/or peppers evenly on pizza crust.

Bake for 12 to 15 minutes or until cheese is melted and bubbly.

PER SERVING: Calories 333; Total Fat 10.6g; Saturated Fat 4.8g; Trans Fat 0g; Cholesterol 82mg; Sodium 662mg; Carbohydrate 27.2g; Dietary Fiber 5.6g; Sugars 4.3g; Protein 35.8g; Vitamin A 9%; Vitamin C 9%; Calcium 45%; Iron 12%.

Creamy Chicken Risotto Cakes

I'm a big fan of Uncle Ben's® innovative "Whole Grain White Rice" which looks and tastes like white rice, but has all the nutrition of brown rice! This all-in-one dish is a fun variation on chicken with rice on the side. These risotto cakes stick together even better when using day-old cold rice, so it's a perfect use of leftovers.

25 minutes

MAKES 12 CAKES (ABOUT 4 SERVINGS)

1 large egg

6 tablespoons White Puree (see Make-Ahead Recipe #4, p. 51) or baby food carrot puree

2 tablespoons ground flaxseed

2 cups cooked Uncle Ben's® Whole Grain White Rice, Creamy Chicken Flavor

1 cup cooked chicken, diced

1 cup of wheat germ, divided

½ cup plus 2 tablespoons shredded, reduced-fat mozzarella cheese

Preheat the oven to 400 degrees and spray a baking sheet with oil.

In a mixing bowl, whisk together the egg, puree, and flax. Stir in the rice, chicken, 2 tablespoons of wheat germ, and ½ cup of the mozzarella cheese. Scoop about ¼ cup of the rice mixture onto the prepared baking sheet, slightly flattening into cakes. Sprinkle the tops of the cakes evenly with the remaining wheat germ and then mozzarella cheese.

Spray the tops of the pancakes with oil and bake for 20 to 25 minutes until cheese is melted and lightly browned.

Serve immediately, or let cool and store in a plastic bag in the freezer for use within 3 months (simply heat through when ready to eat).

PER SERVING: Calories 300; Total Fat 8.2g; Saturated Fat 2.1g; Trans Fat 0g; Cholesterol 108mg; Sodium 487mg; Carbohydrate 28.5g; Dietary Fiber 4.9g; Sugars 2.3g; Protein 29.8g; Vitamin A 6%; Vitamin C 8%; Calcium 17%; Iron 13%.

Texas Two-Step Tortillas

Yee-haw! This dish takes less than 2 minutes to cook! My family loves to mix in their own additions and wrap it up themselves, and if kids help make it, they're more likely to love it!

2 minutes

MAKES 8 TORTILLAS (4 SERVINGS)

½ cup store-bought BBQ sauce

¼ cup White Puree (see Make-Ahead Recipe #4, p. 51) or baby food mixed green vegetable puree

2 tablespoons tomato paste

2 tablespoons ground flaxseed or wheat germ

12 ounces cooked, shredded chicken (about 3 cups)

8 (6-inch round) corn tortillas (white or yellow)

Combine all ingredients (except tortillas) in a microwave-safe bowl and microwave on high for one minute or until heated through. Set aside.

Wrap tortillas in damp paper towels and microwave on high for 30 seconds.

Place each warm tortilla on a plate and evenly distribute the chicken mixture in the middle of each tortilla. Fold over and serve.

PER SERVING: Calories 280; Total Fat 4.7g; Saturated Fat 0.4g; Trans Fat 0g; Cholesterol 70mg; Sodium 353mg; Carbohydrate 31.2g; Dietary Fiber 3.9g; Sugars 3.7g; Protein 29.1g; Vitamin A 3%; Vitamin C 11%; Calcium 1%; Iron 12%.

Flax

Flax was one of the original "medicines" used by Hippocrates, and no wonder: it has heaps of omega-3 fatty acids, may ward off cancer, improves immunity, boosts brain development, helps combat skin conditions, regulates blood sugar levels, and helps you burn fat!

Easy Cheesy Chicken Nachos

20 minutes

Dinner at your house doesn't have to break the calorie bank! This recipe will ensure your kids' friends ask to stick around after school. Give 'em a healthy pomegranate "soda" (p. 246) along with these loaded-up nachos and yours will be the "go-to" house for playdates!

MAKES 4 SERVINGS

12 (6-inch round) corn tortillas (white or yellow) or 96 Make-Ahead "Instant" Tortilla Chips (p. 75)

2 tablespoons extra virgin olive oil

1 tablespoon ground flaxseed

2 tablespoons taco seasoning mix (packaged or Make-Ahead "Instant" Taco Seasoning Recipe, p. 76)

¼ cup tomato paste

¼ cup Orange Puree (see Make-Ahead Recipe #2, p. 45) or baby food carrot puree

2 cups cooked chicken, shredded

½ cup shredded, reduced-fat Mexican or cheddar cheese

Optional garnish: plain Greek yogurt, chopped jalapeños, salsa

Preheat oven to 400 degrees.

If not using Make-Ahead "Instant" Tortilla Chips, brush or spray both sides of the tortillas with oil. Stack 6 of them together and, using kitchen scissors, cut the stack into 8 triangles. Repeat with the final 6 tortillas, for a total of 96 chips. Scatter the chips in a single layer onto a large cookie sheet and sprinkle them evenly with the flax and taco seasoning. Bake for about 10 minutes, or until lightly browned and crispy. Remove from oven and transfer to an ovenproof serving bowl or casserole dish.

In a mixing bowl, combine the tomato paste, puree, and cooked chicken. Spoon the chicken mixture evenly over the crispy corn chips, top with cheese, and bake until chicken is warmed through and cheese is melted, about 7 to 10 minutes.

Top with optional garnishes and serve warm.

PER SERVING: Calories 438; Total Fat 11.3g; Saturated Fat 2.8g; Trans Fat 0g; Cholesterol 103mg; Sodium 642mg; Carbohydrate 44.8g; Dietary Fiber 5.3g; Sugars 3.9g; Protein 41.4g; Vitamin A 32%; Vitamin C 9%; Calcium 22%; Iron 17%.

{ Sneaky shortcut }

In a pinch? Use environmentally friendly paper goods.

Chicken Parm Pops

Chicken nuggets on a stick get lots of smiles (and gives you a chance to sneak in a few more nutrients). They are equally yummy whether you use my superfast One-Step Chicken Nuggets (p. 159) or your favorite store-bought ones.

12 minutes

MAKES 4 SERVINGS

1 package (about 14) fully cooked chicken nuggets or **One-Step Chicken Nuggets** (p. 159)

½ cup store-bought tomato sauce

¼ cup Orange Puree (see Make-Ahead Recipe #2, p. 45) or baby food squash or carrot puree

1 cup shredded, reduced-fat mozzarella cheese

Optional: 14 skewers or craft sticks

Preheat oven to 375 degrees and spray a baking sheet with oil.

In a mixing bowl, combine tomato sauce and puree. Dip one side of each nugget in the sauce mixture, place on the prepared baking sheet, then sprinkle with about a tablespoon of cheese. Bake for 10 to 12 minutes until cheese is lightly browned and bubbly. If using, insert a skewer or craft stick into each nugget and serve.

PER SERVING: Calories 196; Total Fat 9.4g; Saturated Fat 3g; Trans Fat 0g; Cholesterol 36mg; Sodium 680mg; Carbohydrate 8.4g; Dietary Fiber 1.5g; Sugars 2.8g; Protein 18.5g; Vitamin A 21%; Vitamin C 5%; Calcium 21%; Iron 4%.

Chicken Sausage Skillet

I love skillet dinners with only one pan to clean, so much so that I even serve them right in the skillet! Here, chicken sausages add all the flavor you need, and the pasta cooks itself in the simmering sauce. All of which means you'll have more time to catch up with your family after a long day.

MAKES 4 SERVINGS

1 tablespoon extra virgin olive oil

½ cup fresh or frozen chopped onion

4 fully cooked chicken sausages, chopped

1 cup store-bought marinara sauce

½ cup White Puree (see Make-Ahead Recipe #4, p. 51) or baby food carrot or sweet potato puree

1 cup chicken broth, reduced sodium

6 ounces (about 2 cups) dry, uncooked corkscrew or fusilli pasta

½ cup shredded, reduced-fat cheddar cheese

Heat the oil over medium in a deep skillet or earthenware pot. Add the onions and sausages and cook until they are lightly browned, about 10 minutes. Add the marinara sauce, puree, chicken broth, and uncooked pasta, and stir to combine.

Bring to boil and then reduce to simmer, cover, and cook for 30 minutes, stirring occasionally. Add cheese on top, do *not* stir again; cover for about 5 minutes until cheese is melted. Serve hot, right in the skillet!

PER SERVING: Calories 333; Total Fat 14.1g; Saturated Fat 4.2g; Trans Fat 0g; Cholesterol 60mg; Sodium 859mg; Carbohydrate 35.5g; Dietary Fiber 4.5g; Sugars 7.8g; Protein 20.2g; Vitamin A 18%; Vitamin C 11%; Calcium 24%; Iron 13%.

Quicker-Than-Take-Out Chinese Orange Chicken

*Traditional orange chicken is first deep-fried, then stir-fried in a lightly
sweet, soy-based sauce flavored with chopped, dried orange peels.
This version nixes the fatty frying and you can cook it in 9 minutes flat.
It truly is quicker than take-out and just as good.*

MAKES 4 SERVINGS

1 pound uncooked boneless, skinless
   chicken breasts

1 packet (about ⅓ cup) Instant Healthy
   Grain Original Cream of Wheat®,
   unsweetened

¼ cup reduced-sodium soy sauce

1 cup orange juice

½ teaspoon ground ginger

½ teaspoon garlic powder

½ cup Orange Puree (see Make-Ahead
   Recipe #2, p. 45) or baby food carrot
   puree

2 tablespoons canola or vegetable oil

Optional: 2 tablespoons sesame seeds

Cut chicken into chunks, easily done using
kitchen scissors. Place chicken chunks in a
plastic zip-top bag. Pour Cream of Wheat
into the plastic bag, seal, and shake to coat
chicken chunks evenly.

In a mixing bowl, whisk together the
soy sauce, orange juice, ginger, garlic powder, and Orange Puree.

Add oil to large skillet and heat over
medium. Add chicken, turning occasionally,
about 2 minutes each side, until lightly
browned. Add sauce mixture to skillet, stir
to coat chicken, and increase heat to bring
to a boil. Reduce to simmer, and cover,
cooking for about 5 minutes or until chicken
is cooked through.

Sprinkle with sesame seeds before serving, if desired. This dish goes well served over brown or whole grain white rice.

PER SERVING: Calories 239; Total Fat 8.7g; Saturated Fat 0.5 g; Trans Fat 0g; Cholesterol 60mg; Sodium 879mg; Carbohydrate 16.2g; Dietary Fiber 0.8g; Sugars 6.5g; Protein 25.5g; Vitamin A 31%; Vitamin C 32%; Calcium 1%; Iron 12%.

Nutrition Burst

Fiber

Fiber keeps kids regular and fills them up. Wondering if your family is getting enough? Remember the Rule of Age Plus Five: Add five to your child's age in order to get her minimum daily grams. For example, a 4-year-old should get at least 9 grams of fiber a day. One way to do just that: select a breakfast cereal with a minimum of 5 grams of fiber per serving. Other good (and yummy) sources of fiber: raspberries, blackberries, pears, oranges, apples, beans, lentils, chickpeas, whole-grain bread and pasta, oatmeal, popcorn, nuts, ground flaxseed, sweet potatoes, and green peas.

One-Step Chicken Nuggets

For a quick shortcut to homemade nuggets, keep the dry ingredients mixed up in a plastic bag so you're ready to go any night of the week.

MAKES 4 SERVINGS

Cooking spray oil

1 pound uncooked boneless, skinless chicken breasts

1 packet (about ⅓ cup) Instant Healthy Grain Original Cream of Wheat®, unsweetened

1 teaspoon onion powder

¾ teaspoon salt

½ teaspoon paprika

Preheat oven to 425 degrees and generously coat baking sheet with cooking spray oil.

Cut chicken into chunks, easily done using kitchen scissors. Combine all ingredients except chicken in zip-top plastic bag, seal, and shake to mix. Add chicken pieces, seal, and shake to coat chicken evenly. Remove chicken pieces and place on prepared baking sheet. Generously coat chicken with more cooking spray and bake for 12 to 14 minutes or until browned and cooked through.

PER SERVING: Calories 128; Total Fat 1.6g; Saturated Fat 0g; Trans Fat 0g; Cholesterol 60mg; Sodium 726mg; Carbohydrate 6g; Dietary Fiber 0.2g; Sugars 0.2g; Protein 23.8g; Vitamin A 9%; Vitamin C 0%; Calcium 1%; Iron 12%.

Crispy Coconut-Crusted Chicken

Even though coconut has a "candy-like" quality, it's a natural fruit. It crisps up nicely using my faux-fry oven-baked method, too.

MAKES 4 SERVINGS

1 pound uncooked boneless, skinless, thinly
   sliced chicken breasts

¾ cup bottled soy ginger or Asian ginger
   dressing

1¼ cup butternut squash puree (frozen or
   baby food squash puree)

2 cups shredded flake coconut, sweetened
   or unsweetened

¼ cup dry oat bran

Optional: Skewers* or wooden craft sticks,
   soaked in water

*Note: Don't have skewers in your pantry? No problem. Just follow the directions and use a spatula to flip and remove them from the pan.

Preheat oven to 400 degrees and grease or spray a baking sheet with oil.

Cut chicken into thin strips, easily done using kitchen scissors. If using skewers, thread each chicken tender on a skewer before dipping.

In a mixing bowl, combine dressing and puree. Remove about ½ cup of the dressing mixture and set aside to serve as a dip. Combine the coconut and oat bran in a zip-top plastic bag. Dredge each chicken strip in the dressing mixture, then coat in the coconut mixture and place on the prepared baking sheet. Discard any remaining dressing mixture that touched the raw chicken.

Bake chicken for about 8 minutes, then flip once (using a spatula or lifting from the skewers) and cook for another 8 minutes or until lightly toasted and the chicken is cooked through.

Let cool for about 5 minutes before serving—this helps coconut adhere as it cools. Serve with the set-aside dipping sauce.

PER SERVING: Calories 339; Total Fat 17.8g; Saturated Fat 8.1g; Trans Fat 0g; Cholesterol 60mg; Sodium 660mg; Carbohydrate 18g; Dietary Fiber 1.5g; Sugars 3g; Protein 29g; Vitamin A 90%; Vitamin C 16%; Calcium 4%; Iron 10%.

Sweet Salmon Sliders

I learned about Indian candy salmon on a trip to the Pacific Northwest. It usually requires a tedious 20-day process of curing and drying salmon so that it becomes a consistency similar to jerky, and is alleged to be the way Native Americans convinced their kids to eat salmon. For my version, the maple and brown sugar oatmeal packet adds a gently sweet taste that eliminates any fishy flavor.

9 minutes

MAKES 10 BURGERS (5 SERVINGS)

6 tablespoons Orange Puree (see Make-Ahead Recipe #2, p. 45) or baby food carrot or sweet potato puree

6 tablespoons liquid egg white or 2 egg whites

¼ cup wheat germ

2 packets (about ⅔ cup) instant oatmeal, maple and brown sugar flavored

1 large can (about 14 ounces) wild salmon, drained

10 slider buns or small soft dinner rolls (ideally whole wheat)

Optional toppings: honey mustard, sliced pickles, lettuce, tomato slices

Heat a large skillet or indoor grill pan to medium and brush or spray with oil.

In a mixing bowl, whisk the puree, egg whites, and wheat germ, then mix in the oatmeal and salmon until well combined.

Using damp hands, shape mixture into 10 patties (about ¼ cup sized each). At this point, the burgers may be prepared a day ahead and kept covered in the refrigerator, or frozen. If you are not freezing for future use, proceed to next steps.

Spray both sides of the salmon burgers with oil and place them on the prepared grill pan or skillet. Cook for 4 to 5 minutes on each side, or until cooked through.

Serve on whole grain buns with honey mustard and pickles, if desired.

PER SERVING: Calories 390; Total Fat 8g; Saturated Fat 0.7g; Trans Fat 0g; Cholesterol 28mg; Sodium 849mg; Carbohydrate 52.3g; Dietary Fiber 4.5g; Sugars 12.4g; Protein 29.8g; Vitamin A 28%; Vitamin C 1%; Calcium 12%; Iron 25%.

 **Nutrition Burst**

Salmon

Wild salmon is not only an excellent source of omega-3's, but a concentrated food source of vitamin D (helps calcium absorption and essential for bone and immune health). However, research shows that farmed salmon has only a quarter as much vitamin D as wild salmon. Most canned salmon comes from wild salmon sources.

Crunchy Fish Stick Tacos

If guacamole is a favorite in your house like it is in mine, your family will love these tacos! Mixing in Green Puree to the prepared guac from the produce section not only adds three of the healthiest veggies around, but also a bright, fresh taste.

17 minutes

MAKES 8 TACOS (4 SERVINGS)

1 package (about 16) fish sticks, like Dr. Praeger's®

½ cup prepared guacamole

¼ cup Green Puree (see Make-Ahead Recipe #3, p. 48)

Juice from half a lime

8 (6-inch round) corn tortillas (white or yellow) or 8 taco shells

Optional toppings: salsa, diced tomato, shredded lettuce, shredded Mexican cheese

Prepare fish sticks according to package directions, usually about 15 minutes.

Mix the guacamole with the puree and lime juice until smooth. Place optional toppings in individual bowls.

Wrap tortillas in damp paper towels and microwave on high for 30 seconds to one minute, or warm taco shells according to package directions. Place some guacamole mixture and 2 fish sticks in each taco shell or tortilla, and serve with toppings.

PER SERVING: Calories 385; Total Fat 14.6g; Saturated Fat 2.5g; Trans Fat 0g; Cholesterol 20mg; Sodium 549mg; Carbohydrate 50.5g; Dietary Fiber 4.6g; Sugars 3.3g; Protein 12.8g; Vitamin A 4%; Vitamin C 13%; Calcium 5%; Iron 8%.

Nutrition Burst

Lemon

More than a garnish, lemon acts as an antioxidant to keep cut fruit from quickly oxidizing (turning brown). Sprinkle lemon juice on apple slices and avocado halves or guacamole to preserve their freshness and to add a squirt of Vitamin C.

Swift Shrimp Teriyaki Kebobs

Most kids love shrimp—they're mild in flavor, fun to hold in your hand, and great for dipping. Thread them on a skewer and you have a fast, healthy dinner. You can find peeled shrimp in the freezer section of most supermarkets these days, saving all the time and aggravation of peeling and deveining fresh shrimp.

8 minutes

MAKES 8 SKEWERS (4 SERVINGS)

32 large shrimp (about 1 pound), peeled and deveined

¼ cup reduced-sodium teriyaki sauce

¼ cup White Puree (see Make-Ahead Recipe #4, p. 51)

32 pieces fresh or canned pineapple, about 1-inch squares

8 skewers, soaked in water

Preheat an outdoor grill to medium high, or heat an indoor grill pan to medium high and spray with oil.

In a mixing bowl, whisk together the teriyaki sauce and puree. Set aside half the sauce mixture for dipping. Thread 4 shrimp and 4 pineapple chunks, alternating, onto each skewer. Brush kebobs with the remaining teriyaki sauce mixture (discard any sauce that touched the raw shrimp). Place kebobs on grill and cook for about 8 minutes or until shrimp are done, turning once.

Serve kebobs with remaining dipping sauce over brown rice or noodles.

Quick Tip:

Reach for some pineapple after a workout—it contains the enzyme bromelain, which may provide relief from inflamed or swollen joints.

PER SERVING: Calories 118; Total Fat 1g; Saturated Fat 0.5g; Trans Fat 0g; Cholesterol 116mg; Sodium 524mg; Carbohydrate 15.8g; Dietary Fiber 1g; Sugars 13.9g; Protein 12.3g; Vitamin A 0%; Vitamin C 24%; Calcium 0%; Iron 2%.

Garlic Express Mashers

15 minutes

I've discovered the best shortcut for making homemade mashed potatoes is to use the frozen, chopped, ready-to-steam ones. This recipe is also a timesaver in that it sneaks in a protein—something many moms tell me is lacking on their kid's plates. Plus, the hummus gives it a rich taste and a creamy, buttery texture kids will gobble up.

MAKES 8 SERVINGS

1 package (about 1½ pounds) frozen cut and peeled potatoes, uncooked, such as Ore-Ida® Steam 'n' Mash® Cut Russet Potatoes

3 tablespoons store-bought hummus

1 to 2 cloves garlic, crushed

2 to 3 tablespoons plain yogurt

½ cup low-fat milk, or more, as needed

Steam potatoes in the microwave according to package instructions, about 15 minutes. In a large bowl, mix together hot potatoes, hummus, garlic, yogurt, and milk, and mash with a potato masher until smooth. Add a bit more milk, if needed. Season with salt and pepper to taste.

PER SERVING: Calories 88; Total Fat 0.7g; Saturated Fat 0.2g; Trans Fat 0g; Cholesterol 1mg; Sodium 259mg; Carbohydrate 16.8g; Dietary Fiber 2.1g; Sugars 0.2g; Protein 3g; Vitamin A 1%; Vitamin C 9%; Calcium 3%; Iron 3%.

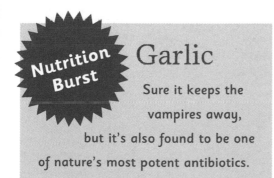

Nutrition Burst

Garlic

Sure it keeps the vampires away, but it's also found to be one of nature's most potent antibiotics.

Mini Muffin Tin Meatballs

This is a time- and energy-saving way to make homemade meatballs—skip the rolling, skip the frying—simply drop a spoonful of the mixture into a mini muffin tin and pop in the oven. Then add them to sauce or stick them right on a toothpick. My kids prefer the latter so they can dip them into a marinara dipping sauce—fun and delicious!

MAKES ABOUT 24 MEATBALLS (4 SERVINGS)

2 tablespoons tomato paste

½ teaspoon dried oregano or Italian seasoning

2 tablespoons ground flaxseed

¼ cup Green Puree (See Make-Ahead Recipe #3, p. 48) or baby food mixed green vegetables

3 tablespoons liquid egg white or 1 egg

¼ cup grated Parmesan cheese

½ teaspoon salt

½ pound lean ground beef or turkey

Preheat oven to 350 degrees and spray a mini muffin tin with oil.

In a large bowl, combine all of the ingredients except the meat. Mix well. Add the ground meat to this mixture and mix until well combined. Using a melon baller or tablespoon, scoop balls into mini muffin tin. Bake for 20 minutes until lightly browned on top.

PER SERVING: Calories 285; Total Fat 13.3g; Saturated Fat 4.8g; Trans Fat 0g; Cholesterol 74mg; Sodium 859mg; Carbohydrate 8.5g; Dietary Fiber 3.8g; Sugars 2.5g; Protein 32.9g; Vitamin A 12%; Vitamin C 15%; Calcium 15%; Iron 23%.

Quick Tip:

Looking for menu inspiration? Serve last night's leftovers for breakfast. (Really.)

Crunchy Panko Meatballs

I've made these as appetizers at parties using vegetarian meatless meatballs, or you can use turkey or beef meatballs. I prefer bite-size smaller meatballs if you're serving on toothpicks.

20 minutes

MAKES ABOUT 24 MEATBALLS (4 SERVINGS)

¼ cup whole-wheat flour

6 tablespoons liquid egg whites or 2 large egg whites

½ cup Panko bread crumbs, ideally whole grain

½ cup grated Parmesan cheese

20 cooked meatballs (frozen, prepared, or Mini Muffin Tin Meatballs, p. 168)

1 cup store-bought marinara sauce

⅓ cup White or Orange Puree (see Make-Ahead Recipe #4, p. 51 or Make-Ahead Recipe #2, p. 45) or baby food carrot puree

Salt and pepper, to taste

Optional: **20 toothpicks**

PER SERVING: Calories 213; Total Fat 7.8g; Saturated Fat 2.8g; Trans Fat 0g; Cholesterol 27mg; Sodium 702mg; Carbohydrate 18.5g; Dietary Fiber 3.1g; Sugars 2.5g; Protein 17.7g; Vitamin A 16%; Vitamin C 16%; Calcium 16%; Iron 8%.

Preheat oven to 400 degrees. Spray a baking sheet with oil.

Place flour in a shallow dish or on a plate. Place egg whites in a bowl next to the flour. In a third shallow dish or on a paper plate, combine the Panko crumbs with the Parmesan cheese.

Roll each meatball in the flour, shaking off excess, then the egg whites, and then the Panko mixture. Press the breading evenly onto each meatball.

Place breaded meatballs on the sprayed baking sheet and bake for 5 to 10 minutes. Turn meatballs over once, then return to oven for another 5 to 10 minutes until golden brown. Combine the marinara with puree and heat in microwave for a minute. Insert a skewer into each meatball, if using, season with salt and pepper to taste, and serve with warm marinara dipping sauce.

Smoky Joe Sliders

This is a smoky twist on a traditional "Sloppy Joe," served up mini-style on slider buns. I especially love the subtle sweet flavor that blueberry adds to BBQ sauce—who knew? Because it isn't bound in a patty, you can also sneak much more nutritious puree into this dish.

MAKES 8 SLIDERS (4 SERVINGS)

1 cup fresh or frozen chopped onion

1 pound lean ground beef

⅔ cup store-bought BBQ sauce

¼ cup tomato paste

¼ cup vegetarian refried beans

¼ cup Purple Puree (see Make-Ahead Recipe #1, p. 43) or baby food blueberry puree

8 small soft dinner rolls, ideally whole grain

Add onions and meat to a soup pot and heat over medium, stirring with a wooden spoon to break up the meat, about 5 minutes or until onions are lightly browned and meat is no longer red. Stir in the remaining ingredients, mix thoroughly, and heat through for 2 to 3 minutes, adding a tablespoon or two of water if you desire a thinner consistency.

Ladle over warm rolls.

PER SERVING: Calories 447; Total Fat 12.9g; Saturated Fat 3.1g; Trans Fat 0g; Cholesterol 65mg; Sodium 514mg; Carbohydrate 48.7g; Dietary Fiber 5.2g; Sugars 13.7g; Protein 35.7g; Vitamin A 18%; Vitamin C 10%; Calcium 9%; Iron 32%.

Onions

More than a garnish on your burger, studies show even 1 tablespoon of onion a day can mitigate the effects of high fat diet. So, add it to meat and lower cholesterol, blood pressure, and blood sugar levels at the same time!

{ Sneaky shortcut }

A slow cooker can actually make dinner prep *faster*—just load it up in the morning so you have dinner ready when you walk in the door in the evening.

Shortcut Shepherd's Pies

Instant brown rice stands in for traditional mashed potatoes in these mini shepherd's pies and it saves you a ton of time. It makes a great casserole or smaller, individual pies.

MAKES 8 MINI PIES OR
ONE LARGE PIE (4 SERVINGS)

1 cup lentil soup, ideally reduced sodium and with vegetables

1 tablespoon extra virgin olive oil

½ cup fresh or frozen chopped onion

1 pound lean ground beef

1 tablespoon whole-wheat flour

2 tablespoons ketchup

1 (8-ounce package—about 2 cups) Uncle Ben's® Whole Grain Ready Rice, chicken flavored

½ cup shredded, reduced-fat cheddar cheese

Optional extra boost: frozen peas or frozen mixed vegetables

Preheat oven to 400 degrees and spray 8 ovenproof ramekins or one 13-by-9-inch glass baking dish with oil.

Measure cold soup into a blender and blend on high until smooth. Set aside.

Heat the oil over medium in soup pot. Add the onions until they are slightly translucent, about 5 minutes; add the beef, stirring to break it up, and cook for about 5 minutes, until the meat is no longer red.

Stir in the flour, then the pureed soup, ketchup, and optional extra vegetables, if using. Mix well. Bring to a boil, and then reduce heat to low and simmer for about 5 minutes.

Divide meat mixture evenly among the prepared ramekins or baking dish, then top each with about ¼ cup of rice (or use 2 cups to top one large baking dish). Sprinkle one tablespoon of cheese on each mini pie (or all the cheese evenly on top of larger pie) to finish, and bake for about 5 minutes until cheese is melted and lightly browned.

PER SERVING: Calories 416; Total Fat 17.1g; Saturated Fat 5.4g; Trans Fat 0g; Cholesterol 75mg; Sodium 352mg; Carbohydrate 29.2g; Dietary Fiber 3.2g; Sugars 2.8g; Protein 31.1g; Vitamin A 14%; Vitamin C 6%; Calcium 22%; Iron 22%.

Nutrition Burst

Lentils

High in fiber, iron, protein, magnesium, and folate, lentils give you a big bang for your buck by keeping you feeling full and energized, lowering your risk of heart disease, and maintaining a healthy digestive tract.

Chili Fusilli

20 minutes

Chili is one of the best hiding places for my purees—I learned this from my very popular chili in my men's book (The Sneaky Chef: How to Cheat on Your Man in the Kitchen). Serving it essentially as a meat sauce over corkscrew pasta gives chili even more kid-appeal, as does the hint of sweetness from the flavored oatmeal packet.

MAKES 4 SERVINGS

1 tablespoon extra virgin olive oil

½ cup fresh or frozen chopped onion

½ pound lean ground beef

6 tablespoons Green Puree (see Make-Ahead Recipe #3, p. 48) or baby food mixed green vegetable puree

2 cups plus 2 tablespoons tomato sauce

¼ cup tomato paste

½ oatmeal packet (about 3 tablespoons), maple and brown sugar flavor

2 to 4 tablespoons chili seasoning mix or 1 tablespoon chili powder

1 can (about 15 ounces) red kidney beans, drained and rinsed*

2 cups cooked fusilli noodles

Salt

Optional garnish: sliced scallions, reduced-fat sour cream, shredded cheddar cheese

Note: If your family objects to whole, visible beans, simply puree them before adding to the chili.

Heat the oil over medium in soup or chili pot. Add the onions until they are slightly translucent, about 5 minutes; add the beef, stirring to break it up, and cook for about 5 minutes, until the meat is no longer red.

Add all of the remaining ingredients (except the fusilli), stir, and bring to a boil over high heat. Reduce heat to simmer for another 10 minutes or until desired consistency.

Divide fusilli evenly among bowls and spoon chili over pasta. Season with salt and more spice, to taste.

Top bowls with scallions, sour cream, and cheese, if using.

PER SERVING: Calories 409; Total Fat 9.3g; Saturated Fat 2g; Trans Fat 0g; Cholesterol 32mg; Sodium 996mg; Carbohydrate 58.7g; Dietary Fiber 10.5g; Sugars 6.2g; Protein 23.3g; Vitamin A 9%; Vitamin C 12%; Calcium 7%; Iron 27%.

Pizza Meatloaf Muffins

Who says meatloaf has to be in a, well, loaf? These individual sized "muffins" are loaded with veggies and whole grains and cook up way quicker than when it's in a loaf pan. The pizza topping makes it even more loveable.

35 minutes

MAKES 8 MUFFINS (8 SERVINGS)

½ cup butternut squash puree (frozen or baby food squash puree)

¾ cup store-bought marinara sauce

3 tablespoons liquid egg white or 1 egg white

1 teaspoon onion powder

1 teaspoon dried oregano

½ teaspoon salt

1 packet (about ⅓ cup) Instant Healthy Grain Original Cream of Wheat®, unsweetened

1 pound lean ground beef and/or ground turkey

⅓ cup shredded, reduced-fat mozzarella cheese, reserved for tops of muffins

Preheat oven to 400 degrees and grease or spray muffin tins with oil.

In a large bowl, combine the puree, ½ cup of the marinara sauce, egg, onion powder, oregano, salt, and Cream of Wheat. Add in the meat and mix until fully combined.

Scoop mixture evenly into prepared muffin tins. Bake 25 to 30 minutes, or until internal temperature is 160 degrees. Remove from oven and spread tops evenly with remaining tomato sauce and top each muffin with about 2 teaspoons of mozzarella. Return to oven and bake for another 3 to 5 minutes or until cheese melts.

PER SERVING: Calories 248; Total Fat 10.3g; Saturated Fat 3.7g; Trans Fat 0g; Cholesterol 68mg; Sodium 713mg; Carbohydrate 10.8g; Dietary Fiber 1.3g; Sugars 4.3g; Protein 27.8g; Vitamin A 52%; Vitamin C 7%; Calcium 10%; Iron 24%.

NO-BAKE PEANUT BUTTER BAR *Sneaky ingredients:* Carrots, sweet potatoes, flaxseed, brown rice (p. 144)

PIZZA POPCORN *Sneaky ingredient:* Flaxseed (p. 216)
MEXICAN HOT COCOA POPCORN *Sneaky ingredient:* Flaxseed (p. 214)

BETTER-FOR-YOU BLACK & WHITE CUPCAKES *Sneaky ingredients:* Cauliflower, zucchini, pears, whole grains, yogurt (p. 199)

VALENTINE'S SOFT SERVE *Sneaky ingredients:* Raspberries, yogurt, avocado (p. 213)

LICKETY-SPLIT LAYER CAKE *Sneaky ingredients:* Flaxseed, spinach, blueberries, pomegranate juice (p. 197)

CHOCOLATE FUN-DO *Sneaky ingredient:* Avocado (p. 218)

IN-A-HURRY BROWNIE COOKIES *Sneaky ingredients:* Flaxseed, spinach, blueberries (p. 201)

CHOCOLATE CHIP COOKIE CAKE *Sneaky ingredients:* Carrots, sweet potatoes, flaxseed, whole grains (p. 205)

Nutrition Burst

Iron

Iron is crucial for brain development.

A chronic deficit can cause learning and behavior problems. Best sources for iron include shrimp, beef, chicken, beans, lentils, chickpeas, tomato paste, soy nuts, raisins, whole-wheat bread, fortified cold and hot cereals, such as whole-grain Cream of Wheat.

Swift Spaghetti & Meatball Pizza

12 minutes

Inspiration strikes in unexpected ways around here! One night the kids were arguing over whether to have spaghetti and meatballs or pizza, so we made both. When I saw them topping their pizza slices with spaghetti, I realized this could be a great new sneaky recipe. (Remember that next time you tell your kids to stop playing with their food!)

MAKES 6 SERVINGS

¾ cup store-bought pizza sauce

6 tablespoons White or Orange Puree (See Make-Ahead Recipe #4, p. 51 or Make-Ahead Recipe #2, p. 45) or baby food carrot puree

1 large (about 12-inch) store-bought pizza crust, ideally whole grain (such as Boboli® whole grain)

1½ cups cooked spaghetti, ideally whole grain, al dente or firm

12 fully cooked meatballs (frozen, prepared, or Mini Muffin Tin Meatballs, p. 168), sliced in half

1 cup shredded, reduced-fat mozzarella or Italian cheese

Preheat oven to 450 degrees and preheat a pizza stone, if using, or spray a baking sheet with oil.

In a mixing bowl, combine pizza sauce with puree. Spread about ¾ cup of the sauce mixture evenly over the pizza crust. Toss the spaghetti in the remainder of the sauce mixture, then scatter evenly over the pizza crust. Top with shredded cheese then add the meatball halves. Bake for 10 to 12 minutes until cheese is melted, bubbly, and golden brown.

Allow to cool a few minutes, then cut into wedges and serve.

PER SERVING: Calories 257; Total Fat 6.6g; Saturated Fat 2.7g; Trans Fat 0g; Cholesterol 13mg; Sodium 440mg; Carbohydrate 36.5g; Dietary Fiber 6.2g; Sugars 2.8g; Protein 16g; Vitamin A 5%; Vitamin C 6%; Calcium 19%; Iron 10%.

Tuna Penne Alla Vodka

This easy recipe is straight from pantry staples and great for those days when you didn't get to the market.

MAKES 4 SERVINGS

8 ounces uncooked penne pasta

⅔ cup store-bought vodka pasta sauce

2 tablespoons White Bean Puree (see Make-Ahead Recipe #5, p. 54)

2 (6-ounce) cans "chunk light" tuna, packed in water, drained

Cook pasta according to package directions. Drain. Warm vodka sauce, puree, and tuna in pasta pot over medium heat. Add cooked pasta, toss to coat, and serve.

PER SERVING: Calories 335; Total Fat 3.1g; Saturated Fat 0.3g; Trans Fat 0g; Cholesterol 46mg; Sodium 574mg; Carbohydrate 48.9g; Dietary Fiber 3.3g; Sugars 3.7g; Protein g; Vitamin A 5%; Vitamin C 10%; Calcium 4%; Iron 16%.

Nutrition Burst

Beans

A high-fiber diet helps control diabetes and maintain healthy blood glucose levels. Just one cup of cooked beans can provide as much as 15 grams of dietary fiber, more than half the daily value (DV) of 25 grams.

Deep Dish Tortellini Alfredo

40 minutes

This one-dish meal has many healthy benefits. By sneaking the nutrient-dense cauliflower/zucchini puree into the already reduced-fat Alfredo sauce, I boosted the volume of sauce, reducing the fat even further. The crunchy topping turned out to be not just a whole-grain addition, but my family's favorite part of the casserole!

MAKES 6 SERVINGS

One 16-ounce jar (about 2 cups) store-bought Alfredo sauce, ideally reduced fat

1 cup White Puree (see Make-Ahead Recipe #4, p. 51)

½ cup liquid egg white or 4 egg whites

20 ounces refrigerated cheese tortellini, ideally whole grain (such as Buitoni®)

Topping:

¼ cup bread crumbs, ideally whole grain

2 tablespoons ground flaxseed or wheat germ

2 tablespoons grated Parmesan cheese

Cooking spray oil

PER SERVING: Calories 245; Total Fat 10.9g; Saturated Fat 5.8g; Trans Fat 0g; Cholesterol 30mg; Sodium 632mg; Carbohydrate 24g; Dietary Fiber 2.6g; Sugars 3.2g; Protein 12.8g; Vitamin A 0%; Vitamin C 13%; Calcium 19%; Iron 5%.

Toss Alfredo sauce, puree, and egg whites in a 2-quart baking dish. Add tortellini and toss to coat.

Add topping ingredients to a zip-top plastic bag, seal, shake, and sprinkle topping mixture evenly over top of casserole. Generously spray with cooking oil and bake for 40 minutes.

Quick Tip:

Put a potted rosemary plant on your kid's desk: the smell will help boost their memory and increase alertness.

No-Boil Baked Ziti

This one-dish wonder has a secret weapon—vegetable juice. It adds eight more veggies in addition to the puree, and also provides lots of bone-strengthening calcium. Zip your lips—your kids will never know.

40 minutes

MAKES 8 SERVINGS

12 ounces (about 4 cups) dry, uncooked ziti pasta

3 cups vegetable juice, reduced-sodium, such as V8®

1 cup store-bought marinara sauce

½ cup White Puree (see Make-Ahead Recipe #4, p. 51) or baby food sweet potato or carrot puree

½ cup part-skim ricotta cheese

¼ cup grated Parmesan cheese

2½ cups reduced fat mozzarella, divided

Preheat oven to 400 degrees and spray a 13-by-9-inch glass baking dish with oil.

In the baking dish, combine all of the ingredients except 1½ cups of the mozzarella (save that for the top of the casserole). Mix well. Top with remaining 1½ cups of mozzarella cheese, sprinkling evenly over the top.

Cover casserole tightly with foil (use nonstick foil or spray regular aluminum foil with oil so it doesn't stick to the cheese) and bake for 30 minutes. Uncover. Bake another 10 minutes or until the top is lightly browned.

Quick Tip:

The secret to health is to eat a rainbow of foods; the more (naturally) colorful the ingredient, the more nutritious it is.

PER SERVING: Calories 330; Total Fat 9.1g; Saturated Fat 3.9g; Trans Fat 0g; Cholesterol 22mg; Sodium 509mg; Carbohydrate 41.8g; Dietary Fiber 3.3g; Sugars 8.9g; Protein 19.2g; Vitamin A 31%; Vitamin C 50%; Calcium 32%; Iron 11%.

Super Simple Microwave Lasagna

No-boil lasagna is one of mt favorite inventions, omitting the most cumbersome part of the process entirely. Couple that with the speed of a microwave, and you now have an everyday favorite you can make in half the time. Just brown the top under a broiler and no one will know you only pressed a few buttons.

22 minutes

MAKES 6 SERVINGS

½ cup White Bean Puree (See Make-Ahead Recipe #5, p. 54) or store-bought hummus*

½ cup butternut squash puree (frozen or baby food squash puree)

2½ cups store-bought marinara sauce

1 cup part-skim ricotta

2 tablespoons grated Parmesan cheese

6 oven-ready, no-boil lasagna noodles

1¼ cups shredded, reduced-fat mozzarella cheese

*Note: Substituting time-saving hummus for my White Bean Puree adds more flavor and a bit more fat to this dish; be sure your family likes the taste of hummus as it doesn't go as unnoticed as the homemade White Bean Puree.

Spray a microwave-safe 8-inch or 9-inch square baking dish with oil.

In a mixing bowl, combine the White Bean Puree (or hummus), squash puree, and marinara sauce. In another bowl, combine the ricotta and Parmesan cheese.

Spread ½ cup of sauce mixture evenly over the bottom of the prepared baking dish.

Place 2 no-boil lasagna noodles on top of the sauce, side by side. Spoon ¾ cup of sauce mixture evenly over noodles to cover completely, then top with ½ cup of the ricotta mixture in small dollops. Gently spread dollops with the back of a spoon. Sprinkle evenly with 2 tablespoons of mozzarella. Repeat with 2 more noodles, ¾ cup sauce, ½ cup of ricotta mixture and another 2 tablespoons of mozzarella. Top with last 2 noodles, remaining sauce, then remaining mozzarella cheese. Cover with wax or parchment paper, tucking ends under baking dish to hold them down.

Microwave on high for 15 to 20 minutes until cheese is fully melted and noodles are tender. (Optional next step: in order to brown the cheese, place baking dish in oven under hot broiler for about 2 minutes.) Let sit about 5 minutes before cutting and serving.

PER SERVING: Calories 305; Total Fat 10.5g; Saturated Fat 4.6g; Trans Fat 0g; Cholesterol 35mg; Sodium 723mg; Carbohydrate 37.5g; Dietary Fiber 4.9g; Sugars 10.9g; Protein 17.8g; Vitamin A 46%; Vitamin C 1%; Calcium 31%; Iron 15%.

Ridiculously Easy Ravioli Lasagna

To me, lasagna is both an art and a craft, neither of which I'm very good at! But ravioli makes this lasagna fail-proof—and fast. Just mix all the ingredients and cover all sins with a blanket of cheese. Perfecto!

MAKES 6 SERVINGS

1¼ cups store-bought marinara sauce

½ cup White Puree (see Make-Ahead Recipe #4, p. 51)

¼ cup baby food carrot puree

1 package (approximately 14 ounces) large frozen cheese ravioli

½ cup shredded, reduced-fat mozzarella cheese

Preheat oven to 400 degrees and coat an 8-inch or 9-inch square baking dish with cooking spray.

Pour marinara sauce and both purees into baking pan. Mix, then add ravioli and gently toss to cover. Top with cheese, cover, and bake for 20 minutes, then remove cover and brown top for another 10 minutes (increase to broil at end if you want a browner top).

PER SERVING: Calories 409; Total Fat 9g; Saturated Fat 3.4g; Trans Fat 0g; Cholesterol 59mg; Sodium 984mg; Carbohydrate 61.5g; Dietary Fiber 5.2g; Sugars 11.7g; Protein 21.5g; Vitamin A 37%; Vitamin C 11%; Calcium 25%; Iron 16%.

{ *Sneaky shortcut* }

Keep the following items in the freezer at all times: bread, a few cooked chicken breasts, frozen veggies and fruits, cookies for unexpected company, and a pound of beef and fish.

Quick Tip:

Texting tweens and TV-watchers need some extra doses of vitamin A, which helps counteract the toxic effects of radiation from home appliances. A key source of vitamin A is carrots.

DESSERT/SNACK RECIPES

Light 'n' Lemony Pound Cake

60 minutes

You might follow the instructions on the cake box to the letter, but where's the fun in that? I veered off the package's directions and added some new flavors (not to mention a big dose of nutrition—Shhhh. . . .). Yogurt gives the cake a gentle moistness, with almost no discernable tanginess. The beans invisibly melt away and blueberries add a deliciously healthy touch. If your kids don't like blueberries, sub in frozen raspberries or leave it plain.

MAKES ABOUT 12 SERVINGS

2 large eggs

⅓ cup White Bean Puree (see Make-Ahead Recipe #4, p. 54)

½ cup low-fat plain, vanilla, or lemon-flavored yogurt

Zest of two lemons

¼ cup unsalted butter, softened

1 box (about 16 ounces) Pound Cake Mix

Optional: 1 cup blueberries or raspberries

Preheat oven to 350 degrees. Grease or spray a loaf pan 9 inches by 5 inches, or other, depending on pan sizes indicated on pound cake package.

Using an electric mixer, beat all ingredients (except berries, if using) on low speed for 30 seconds, then medium for 2 minutes. Pour thick batter into prepared pan and spread evenly. Bake for 48 to 58 minutes* or until a toothpick inserted in center comes out clean. Garnish with berries and serve.

Note: See pound cake package for baking times for varying sized pans.

PER SERVING: Calories 217; Total Fat 9g; Saturated Fat 4.2g; Trans Fat 1g; Cholesterol 46mg; Sodium 137mg; Carbohydrate 32.4g; Dietary Fiber 0.6g; Sugars 17.3g; Protein 3.4g; Vitamin A 4%; Vitamin C 0%; Calcium 4%; Iron 4%.

60-Second Mini Chocolate Cakes

Instant gratification in a cute cup! What kid won't like that? I used little espresso or demitasse cups, but if you don't have those, silicone cupcake molds are adorable, and simple ramekins work well, too. The dusting of powdered sugar adds tremendous visual appeal—remember, we all "eat with our eyes!"

MAKES 6 SERVINGS

2 large eggs

¼ cup canola oil

6 tablespoons baby food prune puree

2 tablespoons ground flaxseed

¾ cup boxed chocolate cake mix (such as Duncan Hines® Moist Deluxe Classic Cake Mix) or ¾ cup Make-Ahead "Instant" Chocolate Cake Mix (p. 64)

Powdered sugar, for garnish

Optional: handful of semisweet chocolate chips

Grease or spray six microwave-safe ramekins, espresso cups, small teacups, or silicone cupcake baking cups with oil.

In a mixing bowl, whisk together the eggs, oil, puree, flax, and cake mix. Pour into prepared ramekins or cups. Drop a few chocolate chips on top, if using.

Microwave (one at a time) on high for 60 seconds (add 10 to 20 seconds if too moist). Dust tops of cakes with powdered sugar when cool.

PER SERVING: Calories 184; Total Fat 12g; Saturated Fat 1.2g; Trans Fat 0g; Cholesterol 70mg; Sodium 146mg; Carbohydrate 16.6g; Dietary Fiber 2.4g; Sugars 8g; Protein 3.9g; Vitamin A 4%; Vitamin C 0%; Calcium 5%; Iron 4%.

Lickety-Split Layer Cake

I fell in love with Nutella® when I first had it in France (they eat it for break-fast!), and once it made its way into our American stores, I couldn't resist finding a way to healthify it! It makes an instant frosting that's definitely got some nutritional value thanks to the hazelnut. If nuts are an issue in your house, you can substitute chocolate or vanilla icing.

36 minutes

MAKES ABOUT 12 SERVINGS

¼ cup ground flaxseed

3 large eggs

½ cup Purple Puree (see Make-Ahead Recipe #1, p. 43) or baby food blueberry puree

1 cup pomegranate juice

1 box (about 18 ounces) chocolate cake mix (such as Duncan Hines® Moist Deluxe Classic Cake Mix) or 3½ cups Make-Ahead "Instant" Chocolate Cake Mix (p. 64)

Frosting:

2 cups chocolate hazelnut spread, such as Nutella®

2 cups reduced-fat cream cheese

Preheat oven to 350 degrees and coat two 9-inch round cake pans with cooking spray; line bottom of pans with wax paper. Coat wax paper with cooking spray; set aside.

In the bowl of an electric mixer, combine flax, eggs, puree, pomegranate juice, and cake mix. Mix at low speed for 30 seconds, then increase to medium for another 2 minutes. Pour batter into cake pans. Bake for 33 to 36 minutes or until a toothpick inserted in the center comes out clean. Cool cakes, then remove from pans and discard wax paper.

For frosting:

Combine chocolate hazelnut spread with cream cheese in a mixing bowl.

To frost cake:

Place 1 cake layer on a plate; spread with ½ cup frosting. Top with remaining cake layer; spread remaining frosting over top and sides of cake.

PER SERVING: Calories 475; Total Fat 17.4g; Saturated Fat 5.1g; Trans Fat 0g; Cholesterol 61mg; Sodium 599mg; Carbohydrate 66.4g; Dietary Fiber 5.6g; Sugars 47g; Protein 15.6g; Vitamin A 20%; Vitamin C 1%; Calcium 36%; Iron 13%.

Nutrition Burst

Pomegranate

This fruit is an antioxidant superpower: it's got 10 times the concentration of immune-boosting antioxidants than other fruits. They also keep bad cholesterol from forming in your arteries.

Better-for-You
Black & White Cupcakes

21 minutes

Cauliflower cupcakes? Sounds as odd as spinach brownies, but in my first Sneaky Chef book, we proved that's not as crazy as it seems. There's not a hint of veggies or fruit lurking within these moist, delicious cupcakes. A final dusting of powdered sugar dresses these babies up nearly as well as less healthy icing.

MAKES 24 CUPCAKES

3 large eggs

⅓ cup White Puree (see Make-Ahead Recipe #4, p. 51) or butternut squash puree (frozen or baby food squash puree)

½ cup baby food pear puree

1 cup apple juice

1 packet (about ⅓ cup) Instant Healthy Grain Original Cream of Wheat®, unsweetened

1 box (about 18 ounces) yellow cake mix such as Duncan Hines® Moist Deluxe Classic Yellow Cake Mix or 3½ cups Make-Ahead "Instant" Yellow Cake Mix (p. 73)

2 tablespoons powdered sugar

Cream Filling:

2 cups ready-made chocolate pudding

1 cup plain Greek yogurt

Preheat oven to 350 degrees and spray 24 muffin tins or line with baking cups.

In the bowl of an electric mixer, combine eggs, purees, juice, Cream of Wheat, and cake mix. Blend at low speed for 30 seconds, then increase to medium for another 2 minutes. Pour batter into muffin tins, filling about two-thirds to the top. Bake for 18 to 21 minutes (or until a toothpick inserted in the center comes out clean). Allow to cool.

To fill:

In a mixing bowl, combine the chocolate pudding with the Greek yogurt.

Pipe the filling into each cupcake using a pastry (or plastic) bag with tip. Garnish with a dusting of powdered sugar.

PER SERVING (1 CUPCAKE): Calories 126; Total Fat 1.4g; Saturated Fat 0.5g; Trans Fat 0g; Cholesterol 30mg; Sodium 168mg; Carbohydrate 24.6g; Dietary Fiber 1.4g; Sugars 14.3g; Protein 3.8g; Vitamin A 3%; Vitamin C 15%; Calcium 8%; Iron 4%.

Nutrition Burst

Vitamin C

This powerful antioxidant is also called ascorbic acid, and is a water-soluble vitamin that cannot be stored or replenished by the body. We lose it in bodily fluids, so it's important to eat foods rich in vitamin C everyday. A single serving of cauliflower provides over half of the recommended daily requirement of vitamin C. Broccoli, cantaloupe, strawberries, oranges, and kiwi also top the list.

In-a-Hurry Brownie Cookies

11 minutes

Need a homemade brownie fix fast? These scrumptious cookies bake up in one-third the time it takes to bake pan brownies. And, they have all the taste of my signature Brainy Brownies, the treats that had pastry chefs scratching their heads trying to figure out how I managed to sneak spinach and blueberries into a fudgy, delicious dessert!

MAKES ABOUT 36 COOKIES

1 tablespoon unsalted butter

¼ cup ground flaxseed

2 large eggs

½ teaspoon cinnamon

¼ cup Purple Puree (see Make-Ahead Recipe #1, p. 43) or baby food blueberry puree

1 box (about 19 ounces) brownie mix (ideally dark chocolate) or Make-Ahead "Instant" Brownie Mix (see p. 74)

Optional: ½ cup white chocolate chips

PER SERVING (2 COOKIES): Calories 96; Total Fat 1.9g; Saturated Fat 0.6g; Trans Fat 0g; Cholesterol 26mg; Sodium 109mg; Carbohydrate 18.5g; Dietary Fiber 1.6g; Sugars 13.4g; Protein 1.9g; Vitamin A 3%; Vitamin C 0%; Calcium 5%; Iron 4%.

Preheat oven to 350 degrees. Line a baking sheet with parchment paper.

Melt butter in a microwave-safe glass or ceramic bowl in microwave on high for one minute (cover with wet paper towel). Set aside to cool.

In a large bowl, whisk together the flax, eggs, cinnamon, puree, and brownie mix. Add slightly cooled melted butter and chocolate chips, if using, and mix until well incorporated (batter will be fairly thick). Drop single tablespoonfuls onto the baking sheet, leaving about an inch between cookies.

Bake for 9 to 11 minutes or until golden brown. Allow to cool. Store in an airtight container or freeze in a sealed plastic bag for up to 3 months.

Chocolate Chip Tricky-Treat Cookies

10 minutes

This recipe makes the most of the instant nutritional boost of pumpkin (remember, it's a fruit!) without overwhelming the taste of traditional chocolate chip cookies. By starting from an instant mix, you can have hot homemade cookies before you can say "boo"—and it's a great use for leftover cans of holiday pumpkin puree.

MAKES ABOUT 30 COOKIES

1 stick unsalted butter, softened

¼ cup plus 2 tablespoons vegetable or canola oil

1 large egg

½ cup canned 100% pure pumpkin

2 tablespoons wheat germ

1 package (about 17 ounces) dry chocolate chip cookie mix or 2¼ cups Make-Ahead "Instant" Chocolate Chip Cookie Mix (p. 63)

Preheat oven to 375 degrees and line a baking sheet with parchment paper.

In a bowl, combine the butter, oil, egg, and pumpkin. Add the wheat germ and cookie mix, and mix until combined. Drop by rounded teaspoonfuls 2 inches apart.

Bake for 10 minutes or until light golden brown. Allow to cool.

Store in an airtight container or freeze in a sealed plastic bag.

PER SERVING (2 COOKIES): Calories 95; Total Fat 6.5g; Saturated Fat 2.7g; Trans Fat 0g; Cholesterol 13mg; Sodium 46mg; Carbohydrate 8.7g; Dietary Fiber 0.8g; Sugars 5.6g; Protein 0.8g; Vitamin A 10%; Vitamin C 0%; Calcium 0%; Iron 1%.

Nutrition Burst

Pumpkin

Go to sleep, pumpkin! Pumpkin is rich in the natural sleep aid, tryptophan.

Butterscotch Crisps

Old-fashioned butterscotch—the flavors of brown sugar and butter—is so reminiscent of the pudding I used to eat as a kid that I was inspired to try my hand at these crunchy cookies. They're so simple to make—you don't even need to crack an egg! The crushed-up crackers add the fun of whole-grain crunch. This recipe goes from the pantry to your mouth in under 20 minutes, making for a quick trip down memory lane!

MAKES ABOUT 60 COOKIES

¾ cup whole-grain Triscuit® crackers, crushed (about 18 crackers)

½ cup whole-grain pancake mix (such as Aunt Jemima® Whole Grain Blend) or Make-Ahead "Instant" Pancake and Waffle Mix (p. 59)

4 tablespoons unsalted butter, melted

½ cup brown sugar, packed

¼ cup baby food sweet potato puree

1 teaspoon pure vanilla extract

Optional: ½ cup butterscotch chips

Preheat oven to 400 degrees and line a baking sheet (or two) with parchment paper.

Pour crackers into a plastic bag and using a rolling pin or your hands, gently crush crackers into coarse crumbs. Add pancake mix to bag, shake, and set aside.

In a mixing bowl, whisk the melted butter with the brown sugar, puree, and vanilla. Add the dry ingredients to the wet and mix just until combined. Add chips, if using.

Drop single *teaspoonfuls* (size is important here) of batter onto the baking sheet, leaving about an inch between each cookie. Bake 8 to 10 minutes, until lightly browned around the edges.

Remove from the pan and let cool. Store in an airtight container or freeze in a sealed plastic bag.

PER SERVING (3 COOKIES): Calories 65; Total Fat 3g; Saturated Fat 1.7g; Trans Fat 0g; Cholesterol 7mg; Sodium 61mg; Carbohydrate 9g; Dietary Fiber 0.7g; Sugars 3.9g; Protein 0.8g; Vitamin A 7%; Vitamin C 0%; Calcium 1%; Iron 2%.

Nutrition Burst

Potassium

Make sure your little athlete powers up with potassium, a key player in maintaining healthy fluid balance, blood pressure, and helping muscles to contract. Some surprising sources are sweet potatoes and white button mushrooms—just five of those have more potassium than an orange. Other good sources: cantaloupe, apricots, avocado, and yogurt.

Chocolate Chip Cookie Cake

24 minutes

Cookie cakes are all the rage with kids these days, and are an unexpected twist on a traditional birthday cake. They're even quicker to make than individual cookies, since you don't have to spend any time scooping out batter. Want another surprise? Sweet veggies and flaxseed hide brilliantly in this seemingly sinful chocolate chip cookie.

MAKES ABOUT 12 SERVINGS

½ cup Orange Puree (see Make-Ahead Recipe #2, p. 45) or baby food carrot puree

¼ cup ground flaxseed

½ cup canola or grapeseed oil

2¾ cups Make-Ahead "Instant" Chocolate Chip Cookie Mix (p. 63) or 1 package (about 17 ounces) dry chocolate chip cookie mix

Optional: chocolate sprinkles, frosting

Preheat oven to 375 degrees and line a pizza pan (about 12 or 14 inches in diameter) with parchment paper.

In a mixing bowl, mix the puree, flax, and oil, then mix in the cookie mix. Press batter evenly into prepared pizza pan and bake for 22 to 24 minutes or until light golden brown. Add sprinkles, if using, immediately when cookie is hot out of the oven. Allow to cool completely before adding frosting or other decorations.

Cut into wedges to serve.

PER SERVING: Calories 206; Total Fat 12.7g; Saturated Fat 3.1g; Trans Fat 0g; Cholesterol 0mg; Sodium 115mg; Carbohydrate 22.6g; Dietary Fiber 2.4g; Sugars 14.4g; Protein 1.8g; Vitamin A 7%; Vitamin C 1%; Calcium 1%; Iron 2%.

Anyone-Can-Make Crepes— Chocolate

You don't have to be a native Parisian to make homemade crepes. They're as easy as pancakes! Not only are crepes surprisingly simple, they are also extremely versatile—you can fill them with most anything. I purposely went easy on the sugar here, since they are filled with such sweet ingredients.

MAKES 4 CREPES

½ cup Purple Puree (see Make-Ahead Recipe #1, p. 43) or baby food blueberry or prune puree

2 large eggs

1 tablespoon unsweetened cocoa powder

1 tablespoon ground flaxseed

¼ cup whole-grain pancake mix (such as Aunt Jemima® Whole Grain Blend) or Make-Ahead "Instant" Pancake and Waffle Mix (p. 59)

2 tablespoons water

Lightly grease or spray an 8-inch or 9-inch nonstick pan with oil.

In a mixing bowl, whisk together the puree, eggs, cocoa powder, flax, pancake mix, and 2 tablespoons of water (unlike pancakes, you don't want any lumps in crepe batter).

Heat pan over medium. Pour in ¼ cup of batter into prepared pan; tilt the pan with a circular motion so that the batter coats the surface evenly. Cook the crepe for 1 to 2 minutes until edges look golden and top looks dryer, then loosen with a spatula, turn and cook the other side for 1 minute.

Remove crepe to plate and set aside until ready to fill. Or, crepes can be made in advance, stacked between sheets of wax paper, wrapped in plastic, and stored refrigerated for 3 days or frozen for 3 months (thaw before using).

Brush or spray oil on pan before making each crepe.

PER SERVING: Calories 195; Total Fat 3.9g; Saturated Fat 0.9g; Trans Fat 0g; Cholesterol 108mg; Sodium 132mg; Carbohydrate 36.3g; Dietary Fiber 4.5g; Sugars 19.6g; Protein 5.6g; Vitamin A 10%; Vitamin C 11%; Calcium 4%; Iron 6%.

Chocolate Banana Filling

¼ cup chocolate syrup

¼ cup Purple Puree (see Make-Ahead Recipe #1, p. 43) or baby food blueberry or prune puree

2 large, ripe bananas, sliced

Optional: powdered sugar

Mix the chocolate syrup and puree in a bowl. Place banana slices down the center of each crepe. Fold sides in over banana slices and turn over on the plate, seam side down. Drizzle about 2 tablespoons of chocolate syrup mixture over each crepe. Dust with powdered sugar, if using.

3 minutes

Anyone-Can-Make Crepes—Strawberry

MAKES 4 CREPES

½ cup Orange Puree (See Make-Ahead Recipe #2, p. 45) or baby food carrot puree

2 large eggs

1 teaspoon pure vanilla extract

1 tablespoon ground flaxseed

¼ cup whole-grain pancake mix (such as Aunt Jemima® Whole Grain Blend) or Make-Ahead "Instant" Pancake and Waffle Mix (p. 59)

2 tablespoons water

Lightly grease or spray an 8-inch or 9-inch nonstick pan with oil.

In a mixing bowl, whisk together the puree, eggs, vanilla, flax, pancake mix, and 2 tablespoons of water (unlike pancakes, you don't want any lumps in crepe batter).

Heat pan over medium. Pour in ¼ cup of batter into prepared pan; tilt the pan with a circular motion so that the batter coats the surface evenly. Cook the crepe for 1 to 2 minutes until edges look golden and top looks dryer, then loosen with a spatula, turn and cook the other side for 1 minute.

Remove crepe to plate and set aside until ready to fill. Or, crepes can be made in advance, stacked between sheets of wax paper, wrapped in plastic, and stored refrigerated for 3 days or frozen for 3 months (thaw before using).

Brush or spray oil on pan before making each crepe.

Strawberry Filling

¼ cup all-fruit strawberry jam

¼ cup Orange Puree (see Make-Ahead Recipe #2, p. 45) or baby food carrot puree

2 tablespoons ground flaxseed

1½ cups sliced fresh or frozen strawberries

Optional: powdered sugar

Mix the jam, puree, flax, and berries in a bowl. Place one quarter of the mixture down the center of each crepe. Fold sides in over filling and turn over on the plate, seam side down. Dust with powdered sugar, if using.

Chocolate Peanut Butter Cup Candies

I can't think of a better combination than peanut butter and chocolate. In fact, it's such a weakness of mine that I try not to keep that type of candy in the house. But one evening, I had a craving and made a batch of these. I actually ate some before they fully froze! It's one indulgence that I didn't have to feel guilty about—they're packed with flax and veggies.

**MAKES ABOUT 24 MINI CANDIES
OR 12 LARGER CANDIES**

2½ cups semisweet chocolate chips, divided

½ cup creamy peanut butter

½ cup Orange Puree (see Make-Ahead Recipe #2, p. 45) or baby food carrot puree

¼ cup ground flaxseed

¼ cup powdered sugar

Line a muffin tin (mini or regular sized) with baking cups or paper liners.

Melt 1¼ cups of the chocolate chips in a double boiler, a metal bowl over simmering water, or in a microwave, checking every 15 seconds. Stir melted chocolate until smooth. Spoon about one teaspoon melted chocolate into mini baking cups or two teaspoons of chocolate into regular sized cups. With the spoon or a pastry brush, draw the chocolate up the sides of the cups almost to the top. Cool in the refrigerator for a few minutes while you prepare the peanut butter.

In a mixing bowl, combine the peanut butter, puree, flax, and powdered sugar.

Place about one teaspoon of the peanut butter mixture over the chocolate for mini baking cups or two teaspoons of peanut butter mixture into regular sized cups.

Melt the remaining chocolate, and spoon over peanut butter.

Freeze for a minimum of one hour. Serve frozen or slightly thawed.

PER SERVING (2 MINI CANDIES): Calories 274; Total Fat 16g; Saturated Fat 7g; Trans Fat 0g; Cholesterol 0mg; Sodium 55mg; Carbohydrate 30.5g; Dietary Fiber 3.7g; Sugars 25.1g; Protein 4.6g; Vitamin A 8%; Vitamin C 1%; Calcium 0%; Iron 2%.

Choco-licious Pudding Pops

Chocolate pudding in any form is a winner . . . put it on a stick and it becomes a champion dessert! Don't be alarmed by the prunes (let's call them "dried plums"). They actually make the chocolate taste more chocolaty. Plus, they're a good source of fiber and potassium, and they help increase iron absorption in the body.

MAKES ABOUT 6 POPSICLES

1 cup ready-made chocolate pudding

¼ cup plain yogurt

½ cup baby food prune puree

6 Popsicle molds and sticks

In a mixing bowl, combine chocolate pudding, yogurt, and puree. Mix well. Spoon into Popsicle molds, insert stick, and freeze for at least 3 hours.

PER SERVING (1 POP): Calories 59; Total Fat 1.2g; Saturated Fat 0.7g; Trans Fat 0g; Cholesterol 5mg; Sodium 53mg; Carbohydrate 10.8g; Dietary Fiber 0.4g; Sugars 8.4g; Protein 1.9g; Vitamin A 2%; Vitamin C 1%; Calcium 5%; Iron 0%.

Valentine's Soft Serve

For homemade ice cream in a hurry, whip out your mini food processor. (Really!) If you use less liquid than you would for a smoothie, you'll end up with a great soft-serve consistency. Put it in a cone or parfait glass and your kids will be screaming for it in minutes!

MAKES 2 SERVINGS

1 cup frozen raspberries, no added syrup or sugar

½ cup strawberry or raspberry yogurt

2 tablespoons ripe avocado

1 to 2 tablespoons sugar

Optional: 2 wafer ice cream cones

Put all ingredients in a food processor and puree on high (add a little more yogurt if needed to make a smooth, thick consistency). Serve in an ice-cream cone or parfait glass. If you desire harder ice cream, freeze for at least 30 minutes.

PER SERVING: Calories 106; Total Fat 2.5g; Saturated Fat 0.5g; Trans Fat 0g; Cholesterol 1mg; Sodium 31mg; Carbohydrate 19.5g; Dietary Fiber 2.7g; Sugars 13.6g; Protein 2.5g; Vitamin A 3%; Vitamin C 12%; Calcium 5%; Iron 0%.

Nutrition Burst

Raspberries

Of all the fruits, raspberries pack the most fiber into the fewest calories. They're also higher in folic acid and zinc than most fruits. It is difficult to wash raspberries thoroughly, making pesticides a concern, so go for organic.

Mexican Hot Cocoa Popcorn

Popcorn is surprisingly simple to make at home, even without a microwave. With questions arising about the plastics and chemicals in microwaveable popcorn bags, this is a worry-free way to go. Or you can follow the directions at the end of the recipe for safe microwave popping or air-popping. Either way, the result is a delicious, good-for-you treat. The dusting of cocoa will satisfy both the sweet and salty cravings in your house.

MAKES 2 SERVINGS (ABOUT 3½ CUPS POPPED CORN EACH SERVING)

½ teaspoon cinnamon

1 tablespoon hot cocoa powder, sweetened
(or 1½ teaspoons unsweetened cocoa
and 1½ teaspoons sugar)

1 tablespoon ground flaxseed

¼ teaspoon salt

1 tablespoon coconut or canola oil

¼ cup unpopped popcorn kernels

Good-quality spray oil

Optional: pinch of chili powder

In a small bowl, combine the cinnamon, hot cocoa powder (or cocoa and sugar), flax, salt, and chili powder (if using).

In a large pot with a lid, heat the oil over medium. Stir in the popcorn kernels and shake to coat with oil. Reduce heat to medium low, cover the pot, and cook, shaking the pot often, until the continuous popping sound ends. Transfer to a large bowl, mist evenly with oil, and sprinkle on the cinnamon cocoa mixture. Serve hot.

Alternative Cooking Methods

Microwave: Put kernels in a paper lunch bag, fold over the top, secure it with a piece of tape, and microwave on high for 3 minutes. Mist oil and sprinkle the cocoa and spice mixture (see directions above) over popcorn when popped.

Air-popped: Follow directions for your popcorn machine. Mist oil and sprinkle the cocoa and spice mixture (see directions above) over popcorn when popped.

PER SERVING: Calories 149; Total Fat 9g; Saturated Fat 0.9g; Trans Fat 0g; Cholesterol 0mg; Sodium 296mg; Carbohydrate 15.9g; Dietary Fiber 4.7g; Sugars 0.1g; Protein 3.3g; Vitamin A 2%; Vitamin C 0%; Calcium 4%; Iron 8%.

Quick Tip:

Popping two batches of traditional generic popcorn a week, instead of an equivalent amount of microwave popcorn, can save you about $100 a year.

Pizza Popcorn

It's hard to remember that popcorn is full of healthy fiber and counts as a whole grain (something two-thirds of us don't get enough of). Top it with antioxidant-rich spices and calcium-rich Parmesan, and you've got a fun, excellent snack. Serve this up on your next family movie night!

5 minutes

MAKES 2 SERVINGS
(ABOUT 3½ CUPS POPPED CORN EACH SERVING)

½ teaspoon dried oregano

½ teaspoon dried basil

1 tablespoon ground flaxseed

¼ teaspoon salt

3 tablespoons grated Parmesan cheese

1 tablespoon coconut or canola oil

¼ cup unpopped popcorn kernals

Good-quality spray oil

Optional: pinch of red pepper flakes

In a small bowl, combine the spices, flax, salt, Parmesan, and red pepper flakes (if using).

In a large pot with a lid, heat the oil over medium. Stir in the popcorn kernals and shake to coat with oil. Reduce heat to medium low, cover the pot, and cook, shaking the pot often, until the continuous popping sound ends. Transfer to a large bowl, mist evenly with oil, and sprinkle on the cinnamon cocoa mixture. Serve hot.

Alternative Cooking Methods

Microwave: Put kernels in a paper lunch bag, fold over the top, secure it with a piece of tape, and microwave on high for 3 minutes. Mist oil and sprinkle the cocoa and spice mixture (see directions above) over popcorn when popped.

Air-popped: Follow directions for your popcorn machine. Mist oil and sprinkle the cocoa and spice mixture (see directions above) over popcorn when popped.

PER SERVING: Calories 180; Total Fat 10.9g; Saturated Fat 2g; Trans Fat 0g; Cholesterol 6mg; Sodium 410mg; Carbohydrate 14.9g; Dietary Fiber 3.8g; Sugars 0.1g; Protein 5.8g; Vitamin A 4%; Vitamin C 1%; Calcium 12%; Iron 5%.

Chocolate Fun-Do

We went to a popular fondue restaurant for Emily's birthday, and that set us on a fondue frenzy! There's something irresistible about dipping chunks of bread and fruit into cheesy or chocolate fondue, and this simple recipe makes a healthy party out of an afternoon snack or dessert. Avocado is the nutritional all-star here with its good fats, fiber, and innumerable nutrients—and it's tasty with chocolate! You can serve this cold as a dip, too.

MAKES 4 SERVINGS

½ ripe avocado

3 tablespoons low-fat milk

1 cup ready-made chocolate pudding

Skewers

Optional dippers: **banana and/or pineapple chunks, strawberries, graham crackers, chunks of pound cake**

Add avocado and milk to a food processor and process on high until completely smooth. Add chocolate pudding and process until combined. Serve as a cold dip, or to serve warm, transfer to a microwave-safe bowl and heat on high for 30 to 45 seconds.

PER SERVING: Calories 112; Total Fat 5.2g; Saturated Fat 1.5g; Trans Fat 0g; Cholesterol 8mg; Sodium 78mg; Carbohydrate 14.5g; Dietary Fiber 1.7g; Sugars 9.6g; Protein 2.9g; Vitamin A 2%; Vitamin C 4%; Calcium 7%; Iron 1%.

Banana Pops

The kids were thrilled to help out with this project—it entertained us for the better part of a rainy Sunday afternoon. Of course, no one waited until the pops were frozen to enjoy these treats!

MAKES 8 POPS

4 graham cracker sheets

2 tablespoons wheat germ

¾ cup creamy peanut butter

¼ cup Orange Puree (see Make-Ahead Recipe #2, p. 45) or baby food carrot puree

4 large bananas, peeled and halved horizontally

8 ice cream sticks or craft sticks

Quick Tip:

Does your child have a peanut butter allergy? Swap it for soy butter or sunflower-seed butter. They deliver about half of our daily vitamin E needs. Other good sources of vitamin E: nuts, avocado, wheat germ, and plant oils.

Line a baking sheet with parchment paper or foil.

Place graham crackers and wheat germ in a plastic bag and using a rolling pin or your hands, gently crush crackers into coarse crumbs. Pour onto a plate and set aside.

On another plate, combine peanut butter and puree. Insert an ice cream stick into the cut end of each banana half. Dip banana halves into the peanut butter mixture until evenly coated, then roll in the graham crumb mixture. Place each banana on the prepared baking sheet and freeze for at least 30 minutes, then transfer to an airtight container or individual plastic zip-top bags.

PER SERVING (1 POP): Calories 194; Total Fat 9.1g; Saturated Fat 1.5g; Trans Fat 0g; Cholesterol 0mg; Sodium 126mg; Carbohydrate 25.2g; Dietary Fiber 3.2g; Sugars 10.9g; Protein 5.6g; Vitamin A 7%; Vitamin C 10%; Calcium 4%; Iron 6%.

CHAPTER SEVEN

Quick, Healthy Fixes for Your Favorite Packaged Foods

At the core of the *Speedy Sneaky Chef* method are my "Quick Fixes" to make packaged, store-bought foods healthier. In this chapter, I've compiled the best and most popular Quick Fixes, updating them with my latest research and new superfoods, as well as a "label alert" for each category to help you choose the healthiest among the many varieties and brands on the shelves.

Quick Fixes for Oatmeal

There are few foods that can get our family off to a solid start as well as oatmeal. Add a bit of delicious puree, and you'll be adding a variety of flavors as well as lasting nutrition. Use quick-cooking oats to make the process even quicker without sacrificing much nutrition. This breakfast provides great fiber and long-lasting energy.

Add any or all of the following boosters to ½ cup of dry oats:

✓ **1 cup milk**
Simply substitute milk for water when cooking the oatmeal.

✓ **1 to 3 teaspoons ground flaxseed**
Make oatmeal according to package directions, adding ground flaxseed with the oats. You may need to add a bit more liquid if the oatmeal seems dry.

✓ **1 to 3 tablespoons peanut butter combined with baby food squash or carrot puree**
Prepare oatmeal according to directions on package. Mix peanut butter and puree into the oatmeal, mixing until well blended.

✓ **1 to 3 teaspoons wheat germ**
Make oatmeal according to package directions, adding wheat germ with the oats. You may need to add a bit more liquid if the oatmeal seems dry.

✓ **1 to 3 teaspoons oat bran**
Make oatmeal according to package directions, adding oat bran with the oats. You may need to add a bit more liquid if the oatmeal seems dry.

✓ **1 cup pomegranate or blueberry juice**
Simply substitute juice for water when cooking the oatmeal.

✓ **1 to 3 teaspoons blanched, slivered almonds, ground in a food processor**
Make oatmeal according to package directions, adding ground almonds with the oats. You may need to add a bit more liquid if the oatmeal seems dry.

✓ 1 to 3 tablespoons nonfat dry milk

Prepare oatmeal according to directions on package. Mix dry milk into the oatmeal, mixing until well blended.

Label Alert: Oats

Look for oatmeal without high-fructose corn syrup or artificial colors or flavors. "Instant," "quick-cooking," and "old-fashioned" are generally about equal in nutrition; "steel cut oats" take considerably longer to cook and have a very different, chewier texture, but may be a nice weekend treat. While rolled oats are steamed, rolled, re-steamed, and toasted, steel cut oats do not go through this additional processing, so they are arguably healthier. Steel cut oats maintain their natural flavor and texture—just be prepared to cook them for about 40 minutes, or overnight in a slow cooker vs. 2 minutes for quick-cooking oats!

Nutrition Burst

Oats

Oats are recognized for their cholesterol-lowering benefits, and were the first grain approved to carry a health claim related to their help in fighting heart disease. Oats are like soluble-fiber "taxis" that escort bad cholesterol and carry it from your body. A daily bowl of oatmeal can reduce your total cholesterol by as much as 25 percent.

Nutrition Burst

Almonds

A snack with staying power, a one-ounce serving of almonds is packed with vitamin E, magnesium, fiber, phosphorous, monounsaturated fat, protein, potassium, calcium, and iron—all of which team up to lower your risk of heart disease.

Quick Fixes for Cold Cereal

Surveys find that cold cereal tops the list of most common breakfast foods (and snacks), with almost half of Americans starting their day with a bowl. We all know kids beg for colorful, high-sugar cereals, and this is a particularly tough battle to win. Some companies are doing a better job of reducing sugar and adding fiber, but we can push that movement along even faster with these tricks. Here are some win-win solutions so you get the lower-sugar, higher-fiber cereals eaten, and your kids get a little of their favorite variety.

✓ Mix low-sugar, whole-grain cereal with look-alike higher-sugar cereal. Put your kids' favorite cereal on top, then bury the healthier cereal underneath in the bowl (or mix them right in the kids' favorite box of cereal). For example:
- Top Frosted Flakes® with Wheaties®
- Top Frosted Mini-Wheats® with unsweetened Shredded Mini-Wheats®

✓ Make fun, fruity milks by adding mashed or pureed blueberries or strawberries to milk. Tip: Frozen fruit, thawed, works best.

✓ Add your own fun "prize" as an incentive to eat lower-sugar, higher-fiber cereals—kids will want the healthy cereal as much as the junkier cereal that usually contains the prize! Fun prizes include stickers, press-on tattoos, plastic worms and spiders, etc.

✓ Top cereal with "Sneaky Chef Nutrition Sprinkles": mix equal parts ground flaxseed or wheat germ, unsweetened cocoa powder, and cinnamon. Tell kids this turns milk chocolaty and they may go for it!

Label Alert: Cold Cereal

Read the ingredient list—don't simply rely on the front of the box for nutrition information! Many cereals scream "whole grain" on the front, but there's actually very little whole grain inside. Look for cereals with "reduced sugar" (but avoid those with sucralose or aspartame, artificial sweeteners); look for cereals with a minimum of 3 grams of fiber per serving, and ideally 5+ grams of fiber per serving, and less than 190 calories per serving. Avoid artificial food dye, high-fructose corn syrup, and hydrogenated oils.

As a general rule, the fewer ingredients the better! Look for "whole" among the first words in the ingredient list, indicating whole grains that are healthier than refined grains. If you see milled corn, corn meal, wheat flour, or rice in the list of ingredients, you're getting a mixture of whole and refined grains. The most healthful cereals are made with whole grains and not much else, but be careful of too much fiber (8+ grams) per serving, which can overwhelm young digestive systems.

Quick Fixes for Boxed
Mac 'n' Cheese

Mac 'n' cheese continues to be one of the favorite American comfort foods. You can never have enough varieties to choose from of this cheesy, creamy family staple.

A note about food dyes:
New research is casting concern about the potential effect of food dyes on our children's health. While waiting for the outcome of the studies, why not err on the side of caution and choose brands without these additives, or simply get the "white" version as opposed to the colored "yellow" version.

You can mix a total of about ½ cup of the following into each 6-ounce box of mac 'n' cheese. Prepare macaroni and cheese according to directions on package. Add booster and mix until well blended:

✓ 2 to 4 tablespoons store-bought hummus (this adds a definite flavor, so be careful)

✓ 2 to 4 tablespoons butternut squash puree (frozen or baby food squash puree)
This works well with an extra slice of American cheese or ¼ cup grated cheddar melted into the sauce to help mask the squash, which has a bit more distinguishable taste than pureed carrots or sweet potatoes.

✓ 2 to 4 tablespoons Orange Puree (see Make-Ahead Recipe #2, p. 45)

✓ 2 to 4 tablespoons White Puree (see Make-Ahead Recipe #4, p. 51)
This works well with an extra slice of American cheese or ¼ cup grated cheddar melted into the sauce to help mask the cauliflower, which has a bit more distinguishable taste than pureed carrots or sweet potatoes.

✓ **2 to 4 tablespoons White Bean Puree (see Make-Ahead Recipe #5, p. 54)**

✓ **¼ cup to ½ cup tofu**
Puree tofu in a food processor until smooth or mash it well with the back of a fork. Add to cheese sauce, mixing until well blended.

✓ **1 to 2 slices American cheese or ¼ cup grated cheddar cheese**
Add extra cheese to the packaged cheese sauce, mixing well until completely melted.

Label Alert: Mac 'n' Cheese

Avoid artificial colors and flavors (yellow versions often have yellow dye); look for "whole grain" on the label and "organic," if possible. Some brands have organic cheese but not organic pasta, so read carefully. Choose "whole grain" over "enriched macaroni" in the ingredient list.

Quick Fixes for Tuna Fish

Nothing hits the spot quite like a tuna sandwich. And because tuna has such a familiar and loveable flavor of its own, you can gradually increase the amount of the nutritious sneaky ingredient over time, as with all Sneaky Chef recipes. Any or all of the ingredients listed below hide beautifully in a 6-ounce can of chunk light or chunk white tuna, packed in water and drained. You can also combine any or all of the following Quick Fixes. Your family will wonder why tuna sandwiches and salads suddenly taste so amazing!

Label Alert: Tuna

"Chunk white" tuna may contain up to three times the harmful mercury of "chunk light" tuna. Choose tuna with "no salt added" and add your own seasonings so you can control the sodium. "Packed in water" contains far less fat then "packed in oil." Avoid added vegetable broth in tuna if you want to reduce sodium. Look for the sodium level to be below 400mg per serving. Always avoid added monosodium glutamate (MSG), as well as damaged cans or cans that are out of date.

Here are my best quick fixes for tuna:

✓ **Include canned (skinless and boneless) sardines in water**
Sardines have almost no mercury and lots of IQ-boosting omega-3 oils. (Just remember this: "Little fish, big benefits!") Mixing them in with the tuna fish your kids already love makes them an instant nutritional boost. Start by mixing in 2 ounces of sardines per 6 ounces of tuna, and over time, gradually increase the amount of sardines until there are equal parts sardines and tuna (or even more sardines, eventually—this *is* possible!). Continue to stir in mayonnaise or whatever you normally add to your child's tuna fish.

✓ **White Bean Puree**

(see Make-Ahead Recipe #4, p. 54)

Combine 1 to 2 tablespoons of White Bean Puree for every 1 tablespoon of mayonnaise to make tuna salad.

✓ **Wheat Germ**

Start by mixing in 1 tablespoon of wheat germ per 6-ounce can of tuna, along with mayonnaise (and White Bean Puree if desired), and over time, gradually increase to 2 tablespoons of wheat germ.

✓ **Ground Flaxseed**

Start by mixing in 1 tablespoon of flax per 6-ounce can of tuna, along with mayonnaise, and over time, gradually increase to 2 tablespoons of flax.

✓ **2 to 4 tablespoons store-bought hummus (this adds a definite flavor, so be careful)**

Start by mixing in 1 tablespoon of hummus per 6-ounce can of tuna, along with mayonnaise, and over time, gradually increase the hummus.

Label Alert: Sardines

Sardines are naturally very low in mercury and high in essential fatty acid omega-3s. Sardines "packed in water" contains far less fat than "packed in oil." "Skinless and boneless" sardines are milder in taste and a good starting point, but they contain significantly less calcium than sardines with skin and bones. Always avoid added monosodium glutamate (MSG). Look for the sodium level to be below 400mg per serving. "Bristling" sardines are said to have the best taste (among sardine lovers) and mildest aroma; they also contain skin and bones for more calcium and omega-3s. Always avoid damaged cans or cans that are out of date.

✓ **2 to 4 tablespoons butternut squash puree (frozen or baby food squash puree)**

Start by mixing in 1 tablespoon of squash per 6-ounce can of tuna, along with mayonnaise, and over time, gradually increase to 2 tablespoons of squash puree.

Quick Fixes for Canned Pasta Meals in Red Sauce

(such as SpaghettiOs® or Annie's®)

Each of the nutritional boosters listed below has been kid-tested and has proven to be undetectable in taste, texture, and color. Start by adding the least amount recommended of just one of the following nutritional boosters, and then put in a little more every time you serve pasta with red sauce.

Add two or more of the boosters below, up to about one-half cup total per 15-ounce can of pasta meal. Warm through pasta meal and mix in booster until well blended:

✓ 1 to 3 tablespoons nonfat dry milk

✓ 2 to 4 tablespoons White Bean Puree (see Make-Ahead Recipe #5, p. 54)

✓ 2 to 4 tablespoons store-bought hummus (this adds a definite flavor, so be careful)

✓ 2 to 4 tablespoons squash (frozen or baby food squash puree)

Label Alert: Canned Pasta Meals

Avoid canned pasta meals with high-fructose corn syrup. Look for the sodium level to be below 400mg per serving, and for "whole-grain" canned pasta meals.

✓ 2 to 4 tablespoons Orange Puree (see Make-Ahead Recipe #2, p. 45)

✓ 2 to 4 tablespoons White Puree (see Make-Ahead Recipe #4, p. 51)

Quick Fixes for Ranch Dressing

When kids eat raw veggies, they usually just act as a sort of lollipop for the ranch dressing. Kids love the creamy texture and intense flavor. Unfortunately, it's usually loaded with saturated fat and MSG (monosodium glutamate). There are some organic and natural bottled ranch dressings in the market nowadays, without MSG, so take time to read the labels.

By mixing in some plain yogurt, you can increase the volume and cut the fat, as well as add some "friendly live bacteria." Gradually increase the amount of yogurt over time until the ratio is almost even. I've also updated this great recipe with White Puree, and even Orange Puree for a fun, pink party dip variation!

Mix one of the following into 2 tablespoons bottled ranch dressing, and serve as a dip or dressing:

✓ 1 to 2 tablespoons low-fat plain Greek yogurt

✓ 1 to 2 tablespoons White Puree (see Make-Ahead Recipe #4, p. 51)

✓ 1 to 2 tablespoons squash puree (frozen or baby food squash puree) This changes the color to pretty pink .

Label Alert: Ranch Dressing

The biggest culprit in almost every nonorganic ranch dressing is monosodium glutamate (MSG). Avoid it at all costs! Also avoid the high-fructose corn syrup lurking in many dressings, as well as artificial sweeteners, such as aspartame or sucralose. Look for sodium under 400mg per serving. Better brands of ranch dressing are the organic ones.

Quick Fixes for Applesauce

Kids still love applesauce as much as when I was a kid, and now there are even more varieties and natural brands to choose from. The other option is to make your own flavored applesauce by starting with your favorite natural applesauce and mixing in one of the following boosters. Serve in the original little plastic tubs for real authenticity.

Mix one the following boosters into 1 cup of applesauce, and stir until well combined:

✓ 2 to 4 tablespoons pomegranate or blueberry juice

✓ 2 to 4 tablespoons prune, pear, or blueberry baby food

✓ 2 to 4 tablespoons cranberry sauce (no added corn syrup)

✓ 2 to 4 tablespoons plain low-fat yogurt (the French love this combo!)

Label Alert: Applesauce

Berry-flavored is a favorite, but it often uses artificial colors and flavors. Try to choose applesauce that doesn't have such artificial colors or flavors, high-fructose corn syrup, or any other added sweeteners.

Quick Fixes for Store-bought Tomato, Marinara, and Pasta Sauce

While experimenting with store-bought tomato sauce one day, I stumbled upon a secret top Italian chefs have known for centuries: no matter how great a tomato sauce starts off, it only gets better with some secret touches that sweeten it up and lower its acidity. It even cuts back on potential reflux or indigestion that often arises after eating tomato sauce.

Each of the boosters below does just that, as well as one other critical thing: the sneaky ingredients significantly up the nutritional profile of the sauce with extra fiber, vitamins, and minerals. If your family is sensitive to slight color variations, you've got another trick up your sleeve: just add a little canned tomato paste to the sauce. You can mix one or more of the boosters below, up to a total of about ½ cup booster per 1 cup of store-bought tomato sauce.

Add the following boosters, up to ½ cup total, into 1 cup of bottled sauce, mixing until well blended:

✓ **1 to 3 tablespoons nonfat dry milk**
This makes more of a creamy pink sauce, á la vodka sauce.

✓ **¼ cup evaporated milk**
This also makes more of a creamy pink sauce.

✓ **2 to 4 tablespoons hummus**
(this adds definite flavor, so be careful)

✓ **2 to 4 tablespoons Orange Puree**
(see Make-Ahead Recipe #2, p. 45)

✓ **2 to 4 tablespoons White Puree**
(see Make-Ahead Recipe #4, p. 51)

✓ **2 to 4 tablespoons White Bean Puree (see Make-Ahead Recipe #5, p. 54)**
If the sauce becomes too light, simply mix in a tablespoon or so of canned tomato paste to bring the color back to a deeper red.

✓ **2 to 4 tablespoons squash puree (frozen or baby food squash puree)**
If the sauce becomes too light, simply mix in a tablespoon or so of canned tomato paste to bring the color back to a deeper red.

Label Alert: Tomato, Pasta, or Marinara sauce

Choose tomato-based sauces in bottles, not cans. Tomato products in cans can leach the toxic chemical BPA (Bisphenol A) from the lining of the can into the food. Organic tomato sauces contain more than twice the cancer-fighting antioxidant lycopene. Avoid sauces containing high-fructose corn syrup, and choose sauce with less than 5 grams sugar and less than 400mg sodium per serving.

Quick Fixes for Store-bought Chocolate Pudding

Not only do these boosters add great nutrients, but they reduce the overall sugar content of the pudding. You can add sprinkles to distract attention from any texture changes.

Each nutritional booster below mixes into ¼ cup of prepared chocolate pudding:

✓ 1 to 2 tablespoons baby food prune puree

✓ 1 to 2 tablespoons baby food pear puree

✓ 1 to 2 tablespoons low-fat plain Greek yogurt

✓ ⅛ ripe avocado, pureed or mashed thoroughly until creamy

Make sure the avocado is very soft and ripe, but not brown. If it's not ripe enough, it will be too hard to mash with a fork and will require pureeing in the food processor.

Label Alert: Pudding

Avoid "no sugar added" as that usually means there's artificial sweeteners lurking. Avoid high-fructose corn syrup often found in store-bought puddings. "Dark chocolate" pudding has more beneficial antioxidants. Look for "all-natural" puddings.

Quick Fixes for Store-bought Lemonade

Lemonade is one of the most refreshing drinks around. Its combination of tart lemons with just the right amount of sweetener, poured over ice, can make even the hottest of days more enjoyable. When we don't have the time—or the lemons to squeeze ourselves—a good mix or store-bought brand works great.

The teas and juices below work double by adding antioxidants and at the same time reducing the overall refined sugar content of sweetened lemonade.

Mix one of the following with 1 cup of lemonade:

✓ 1 to 2 tablespoons freshly squeezed lemon juice (unless you're starting with freshly squeezed lemonade!)

✓ ¼ to ½ cup orange juice

✓ ¼ to ½ cup pomegranate or blueberry juice

✓ ¼ to ½ cup unsweetened (decaf) black tea

✓ ¼ to ½ cup unsweetened (decaf) green tea

✓ ¼ to ½ cup unsweetened (decaf) herbal or fruit tea

Label Alert: Lemonade

Choose "all-natural" brands with no artificial colors or flavors. Avoid high-fructose corn syrup. Watch out for artificial sweeteners, such as sucralose and aspartame in juices. Ideally, lemonade contains pulp and is "not from concentrate," although this can be difficult to find.

Quick Fixes for Condiments

If you think about it, every time we reach for sandwich ingredients—turkey, ham, cheese—or take just about anything out of the fridge, condiments come out too. Why? Because they add richness and flavor and much-needed texture and moisture to otherwise dry, bland-tasting stuff. But it's precisely because they're so flavorful and moist that they make such good hiding places for our healthy purees! For many condiments, including ketchup, mayonnaise, and mustard, Sneaky Chef purees add a mild natural sweetness that the whole family will actually come to prefer. Orange puree makes ketchup even more delicious! You'll come to find that these same condiments will taste bland and lifeless without them.

Remember, because each ingredient has a different shelf life, don't mix purees into the condiment container or store them in the original container. Just add your fresh or frozen (microwave to thaw) purees to condiments in a mixing bowl before use. It's safe to say these mixtures will keep for up to 3 days in the refrigerator.

Nutrition Burst

Ketchup

Kudos for ketchup!
It really is a vegetable.
It's a good source of lycopene,
an antioxidant which may help
prevent some forms of cancer.
Organic ketchup has three times
as much lycopene as nonorganic.

CONDIMENT	QUICK FIX
Blue cheese dressing	2 parts blue cheese dressing to 1 part plain yogurt or White Puree
Chipotle in adobo sauce	2 parts adobo sauce to 1 part Orange or White Puree
Cranberry sauce	2 parts cranberry sauce to 1 part Orange Puree
French dressing	2 parts French dressing to 1 part White Puree, Orange Puree, or squash puree
Ketchup	2 parts ketchup to 1 part Orange Puree
Mayonnaise	1 part light mayonnaise to 1 part White Bean Pure
Mustard	2 parts mustard to 1 part White Bean Puree, Orange Puree, or squash puree
Ranch dressing	3 parts ranch dressing to 1 part White Puree or plain yogurt; 1 part Green Puree (makes green goddess dressing)
Red horseradish	2 parts horseradish to 1 part White or Orange Puree or squash puree
Steak sauce	2 parts steak sauce to 1 part White, Green, or Orange Puree
Thousand Island dressing	2 parts Thousand Island to 1 part White Puree or Orange Puree

Quick Fixes for Canned Baked Beans

Fiber and nutrient-rich baked beans are packed in a rich sauce that's absolutely loaded with sweet, smoky flavor. That's what makes them a favorite in my house. But, of course, that delicious flavor sometimes comes with a price. In this case, it's usually quite a bit of added sugar, and depending on the brand, artificial flavors, colors, and even MSG. So look for the more natural brands, and to cut the sugar, mix in a healthy portion of, you guessed it, sweet purees! They'll deliver real nutrition with their sweetness, which is the best of both worlds. And that's the heart of the Sneaky Chef method.

Each of the boosters below enhances the nutritional profile of canned baked beans. You can mix in one or more of these boosters at once, but keep the ratio at no more than ⅛ cup per 16-ounce can of beans to remain above suspicion.

Each of the following quick fixes is for 1 (16-ounce) can of baked beans. Add to cooked beans, mixing until well blended:

✓ ¼ to ½ cup squash puree
(frozen or baby food squash puree)

✓ ¼ to ½ cup White Puree
(see Make-Ahead Recipe #4, p. 51)

✓ ¼ to ½ cup Orange Puree
(see Make-Ahead Recipe #2, p. 45)

✓ 1 tablespoon flax or wheat germ

Quick Fixes for Store-bought Salsa

Salsa was made for purees. Talk about a great place to sneak in some real nutrition—and into an already pretty healthy product! It's loaded with spices that act as a great flavor decoy for just about any healthy ingredient, and the acidity of the tomatoes is just begging to be cut with the natural sweetness of a little orange puree. The result is a thicker, richer salsa that clings beautifully to chips and tortillas. My friends, family, and neighbors can't get enough of it when I put out a bowl.

Each of the following quick fixes is for ½ cup of salsa. Add, mixing until well blended:

✓ **2 to 4 tablespoons Orange Puree (see Make-Ahead Recipe #2, p. 45)**

✓ **2 to 4 tablespoons squash puree (frozen or baby food squash puree)**

Label Alert: Salsa

Watch for high sodium content! Go for brands under 200mg per serving.

Quick Fixes for
Store-bought BBQ Sauce

When it comes to chicken, ribs, or wings, barbecue sauce rules (I even use it on my grilled salmon!). Now you can make it thicker, richer, less sugary, and healthier with the addition of some secret juices and purees. A thicker sauce clings better so it won't run off as much during the cooking process. The result is more delicious flavor in every bite, and that's what barbecuing is all about.

Each of the boosters below enhances both the nutritional profile of your favorite bottled barbecue sauce and cuts the sauce's acidity, which makes the sauce naturally sweeter and may help prevent acid reflux as well.

Each of the following quick fixes is for ½ cup of store-bought, bottled barbecue sauce. Add, mixing until well blended:

✓ 2 to 4 tablespoons ground flaxseed

✓ 2 to 4 tablespoons baby food mixed vegetables

✓ 2 to 4 tablespoons Purple Puree (see Make-Ahead Recipe #1, p. 43) or baby food blueberry puree

✓ 2 to 4 tablespoons Orange Puree (see Make-Ahead Recipe #2, p. 45)

✓ 2 to 4 tablespoons Green Puree (see Make-Ahead Recipe #3, p. 48)

✓ 2 to 4 tablespoons White Puree (see Make-Ahead Recipe #4, p. 51)

✓ 2 to 4 tablespoons White Bean Puree (see Make-Ahead Recipe #5, p. 54

Label Alert: BBQ Sauce

Avoid high-fructose corn syrup and high sodium. Go for brands with less than 200mg sodium per serving, and under 10mg sugar per serving.

Quick Fixes for Store-bought Guacamole

We all love to dip deep into creamy guacamole. The quick fixes below do more than enhance the nutritional profile of this party favorite—the hidden veggies add fat-free volume as well. You can also mix in two or more of the boosters below, up to a total of about ¼ cup booster per 1 cup of store-bought or prepared guacamole. Add some smart and sassy dipping sticks, such as crunchy celery stalks, carrots, bell peppers, or your own homemade chips (see Make-Ahead "Instant" Tortilla Chips, p. 75), and you can party hearty!

Each of the following quick fixes is for 1 cup of store-bought guacamole. Add, mixing until well blended:

✓ 2 to 4 tablespoons Green Puree (see Make-Ahead Recipe #3, p. 48)

✓ 2 to 4 tablespoons White Bean Puree (see Make-Ahead Recipe #5, p. 54)

✓ 1 to 2 tablespoons oat bran

Because of the added texture, this quick fix will go over better if something crunchy, like chopped red onion, is also added in as a distraction.

Quick Fixes for Canned, Boxed, or Store-bought Soups

The right soup can be a great start to a healthy meal, especially when you add a couple of tablespoons of my superfood purees. The seasoning is already in place, which is half the battle, so you don't have to prepare it from scratch. A healthy lunch or dinner is made in an instant by simply mixing in some purees with your family's favorite canned, boxed, or even store-bought "fresh" soups. The purees not only add a homemade feel to a packaged food, but they significantly enhance the flavor and nutrition.

Use the following rough guidelines to add to prepared soups—start with about 2 tablespoons of puree per serving of soup (add ¼ cup puree to a can of soup that serves 2).

- -

PUREE:	MIX INTO:
White Bean Puree	**Broth-based soups**
Orange Puree, White Puree, or squash puree	**Tomato-based soups**
Orange Puree, White Puree, or squash puree	**Bean-based soups**
White Bean or White Puree	**Creamy soups**
Green Puree*	**Beefy soups**
Orange, White Bean, or White Puree	**Beefy soups**

*Mix Green Puree with equal parts tomato paste to turn brown first, then add to beefy soup.

Quick Tip:

Toss a bay leaf into soup and you may relieve muscle pain and headaches, as well as keep your blood sugar under control.

Quick Fixes for Peanut Butter

Peanut butter is one of those kid favorites that also, thankfully, happens to have a pretty good nutritional profile. It's nutrient-dense, making it a real energy sustainer in a pinch, and it's high in "good" fat, but at 9 grams of fat per tablespoon, it can also pack on the pounds in kids and adults if overindulged. That's why I've lightened it up with these variations. The additions below will not only add a good amount of nutrients, but lower the caloric density.

There are plenty of peanut butter varieties to choose from that don't contain high-fructose corn syrup or partially hydrogenated oils. These days, you can even get low-fat versions! Then, mix one of the boosters into 2 tablespoons of peanut butter. Stir until well combined. I find it easiest to do this on a plate and mix with the back of a fork. Then, make your sandwich as usual and watch the kids (and their parents) gobble them up!

Let peanut butter soften at room temperature before mixing in the sneaky ingredients below:

✓ **1 tablespoon Orange Puree**
(see Make-Ahead Recipe #2, p. 45)

✓ **1 tablespoon White Bean Puree**
(see Make-Ahead Recipe #5, p. 54)

✓ **1 tablespoon wheat germ**
This is easier to get away with when using crunchy peanut butter.

✓ **1 tablespoon ground flaxseed**
This is easier to get away with when using crunchy peanut butter.

Label Alert: Peanut Butter

Even if a jar of peanut butter claims it has "no trans fats," flip it over and read the ingredients, looking for partially hydrogenated oils. If it's listed, it's in there (although in small enough amounts that the label can still say no trans fats), and every little bit adds up. Also watch for added sugars, keeping sugar below 5 grams per serving. Choose "natural" varieties, ideally without the oil floating on the top (which is a mess to stir in).

Quick Fix for Soda Pop

This is at least a partial easy fix to an enormous problem: the average American drinks an estimated fifty-six gallons of soft drinks each year. That's about 20 ounces per day, 365 days a year! And consider that in the past ten years, soft drink consumption among children has almost doubled *in the United States. This has undoubtedly led to the increase in obesity among kids, among a host of other issues. One can of soda has about ten teaspoons of sugar, 150 calories, and loads of artificial food colors, caffeine, and preservatives. Fortunately, there is a quick fix that will immediately cut this problem in* half.

Rather than forbidding soda at a special occasion party or event, try this trick, which significantly cuts down on the sugar content of the soda:

✓ Mix any soda with plain seltzer. Add as much plain seltzer as you can get away with—work up to 3 parts seltzer to 1 part soda!

Quick Fixes for Sparkling Water

Below are fast recipes for sparkling water mixed with our homemade nutrient-rich fruit juices, and they make an excellent alternative to sugary sodas. (Even the new natural sodas on the market provide too many calories in the form of sweeteners and too much sugar for the waistline and teeth.) I mix the juice and seltzer in small water bottles for the kids to take to school, and they enjoy it even more than traditional juice boxes.

Mix equal parts sparkling water and any of the juices below:

✓ 1 to 2 tablespoons freshly squeezed lemon or lime juice
If desired, add a bit of natural sweetener such as raw sugar, agave, or stevia.

✓ ¼ to ½ cup orange juice

✓ ¼ to ½ cup pomegranate or blueberry juice
Juices, even those without added sugar, are usually naturally sweet enough that you don't need to add any extra sweetener.

Nutrition Burst

Carbonated Drinks

It's not just the loads of sugar that should convince you to break the soda habit. The fizziness in carbonated soda often comes from phosphoric acid, which ups the rate at which calcium is excreted in the urine. (This is not usually found in carbonated water/seltzer.)

Acknowledgments

I look back with total amazement and humility over the last 5 years since the first Sneaky Chef book was published. To say that I am grateful to all the people who have helped, supported, encouraged, and inspired me is nowhere near the level of how I feel. Even though I had a vision, dream, and passion, none of this would have been possible without an amazing group of talented, caring, visionary people.

First and foremost, I am so fortunate to work with the best of the best publishers. Thank you David Steinberger, CEO of Perseus Books Groups, and Christopher Navratil, Publisher of Running Press, for your continued support and smart publishing sense.

I am incredibly fortunate to have the same brilliant team at Running Press since the first Sneaky Chef book: I am sincerely grateful to Executive Editor, Jennifer Kasius, whose superb publishing eye turns out exceptional books; to Associate Publisher, Craig Herman, whose keen sense of marketing brings our books to life; to Art Director, Bill Jones, and interior designer Alicia Freile, whose design excellence makes our books so beautiful and easy to use. Thank you to the entire Running Press team — it is an honor to work with each of you!

Of course, without Joelle Delbourgo and Molly Lyons, my amazing literary agents, I would never have reached this point. Thank you for your encouragement, direction, and great advice on an ongoing basis. And to my publicist Jennifer Prost, for spreading the health across the country!

The mouth-watering food photos in all my books are the excellent work and creative genius of food photographer, Jerry Errico, and five-star food stylist, Brian Preston-Campbell — I love our fun and amazing shoots!

A special thanks to my stepmother, Ulla Chase, for your love and help on recipe development, and to my loving Dad, who always supports me in my endeavors.

I'll always be grateful to my mom, Carol, for your never-ending belief in me and helping me learn the power of superfoods; to my sister, Karen, for always supporting me; to my brother, Larry Chase, and sister-in-law, Brigitte Miner, who have been my partners in crime since the first notion of Sneaky Chef.

I am very grateful to the team at UnitedHealth Group, for all your support; and to the visionary team at New York-Presbyterian Morgan Stanley Children's Hospital for inviting me to contribute and for bringing Sneaky Chef foods into your patients' rooms.

I'd be lost without my awesome digital strategist, Monica Dreger, and amazing brand agents, Brandon Gayler and Marc Ippolito of Burns Entertainment. Special thanks to Ken, Brenda and Jenny Fritz for all your guidance and expertise; to Jean Bukhan, my wonderful test kitchen manager; to Karen Ganz and Sharon Hammer for all your delicious creative input; to recipe testers, Terry Grieco Kenny and Pamela Adler, for your recipe development and assistance with this book.

I am always thankful for the love and support of my inner circle of dear friends — you know who you are and I love you all. And I count my blessings every day for my loving husband, Rick, and our beautiful, brilliant daughters, Emily and Samantha — you are my world.

And finally, thank you, my Sneaky Chefs — you are all amazing! You don't give up, you push on for me, and you are the inspiration that keeps me working every day.

Dear Readers,

Thank you for sharing your time with us, and for making The Sneaky Chef a part of your life. To share your ideas and comments, and for new recipes, tips, special promotions, and appearance dates, please come visit us at:

www.TheSneakyChef.com

I also invite you to share your experience with this method and your own sneaky ideas by emailing me at Missy@TheSneakyChef.com.

Index

M

Recipes Listed by Make-Ahead Ingredients

Notes

Notes

Notes

Notes

Notes

Notes

Notes

Notes

Notes